Vital Signs, U.S.A.

A Cass Canfield BOOK

Books by John Fischer

Why They Behave Like Russians
Master Plan: U.S.A.
The Stupidity Problem and Other Harassments

Vital Signs, U.S.A.

John Fischer

HARPER & ROW, PUBLISHERS

New York
Evanston
San Francisco
London

FIRST EDITION

Library of Congress Cataloging in Publication Data

Fischer, John, 1910 (Apr. 27)–
   Vital Signs, U.S.A.
   (A Cass Canfield book)
   Includes index.
   1. Municipal government—United States. 2. Metropolitan gov-
ernment—United States. 3. Regional planning—United States. I.
Title.
JS341.F57   1975   320.9′73′092   74–15823
ISBN 0–06–011247–6

For my wife, Betty, whose suggestions, encouragement, and patience contributed much to this book.

Contents

Acknowledgments

I owe a special debt of gratitude to the many people, some of whom are mentioned in the following pages, who patiently answered my questions and dug into their files for the information on which this book is based. Much of the research and travel was financed by a grant from the Carnegie Corporation; several of its officers, but especially Eli Evans, gave me invaluable encouragement and advice. Yale University provided me with a Visiting Fellowship and library privileges, and the faculty of its Institution for Social and Policy Studies were good enough to read and discuss with me most of the manuscript—although none of them are, of course, responsible for either the factual material or the conclusions. Several, in fact, disagree with at least some of the arguments set forth here. Finally, I am grateful to Mrs. Edith MacMullen, who helped me with the research during the early stages of the book.

Part of the following material was originally published, in quite different form, in the Easy Chair column of *Harper's Magazine*.

1.

The Real Greening of America

When I was in high school a good many years ago, I came across a little book by Don Marquis called *The Almost Perfect State*—the funniest, warmest, and most humane of all prescriptions for Utopia. Ever since, I have been looking for such a state, and when I was younger and more optimistic I even tried, when the chance offered, to build a small corner of it in one place or another. The results were far from perfect, and I am now willing to settle for something less. Even the Good Society may be too much to hope for, given the ingrained orneriness of human beings. But if enough people keep trying for it, we might—just possibly— come within reach of something that could be called the Almost Good Society.

To many, I realize, even this modest expectation may seem exaggerated. In fact, the one proposition on which most Americans seem to agree these days is that our society is in a mess, and getting worse. That may be the only conviction shared by John W. Gardner, Barry Goldwater, Bobby Seale, the Grand Dragon of the Klan, and the Communist Party. Much of the literature of the last decade—which may be remembered as the Era of Lamentation—has been devoted to documenting the country's woes. And, no question about it, we have plenty to lament: wars, racism, a crumbling environment, schools that don't teach, railroads that don't run, and cities dangerous to live in, to mention only a few items on the doleful list.

Yet a good number of Americans, who are well aware of all these troubles, still believe that something can be done about them. You might call them social inventors. Their common purpose is to find new ways to make the society work better. Some of them have been laboring for years, in the face of much discouragement, to get their inventions into operation—without hope of fame, riches, or any reward except the satisfaction of a job well done. Few of them are known outside their own communities, and until recently most of them were strangers to each other.

Their inventions—a surprising variety of them—are only now beginning to work. Some are operating very well indeed, others just so-so. In both cases they have been largely ignored by the national press. Many of the people benefiting from them are hardly aware of their existence. Worse yet, an experiment of considerable promise in one part of the country often is unheard of in other places that might profit from it. For example, some people in Minnesota have devised an ingenious and effective scheme for managing a metropolitan area: it could be adapted with immeasurable benefit to the San Francisco Bay region, greater Seattle, and half a dozen other metropolises. (Though not, I suspect, to New York.) Nevertheless, scarcely anybody in those places knows anything about it.

Another case in point is Georgia, until recently an embarrassment to the rest of the nation, notorious for pellagra, poverty, and rascally politicians. Who would believe that within a decade or so a handful of Georgians, neither rich nor powerful, could market an idea that now is rapidly transforming the state—and spreading, less rapidly, to other parts of the country? (I didn't believe it until I went to see for myself. An account of what is happening there, and why, is in Chapter 3.)

Still other efforts to build the Almost Good Society, or bits of it, are under way in South Carolina, Jacksonville, Seattle, and dozens of other places I have visited. I had never heard of any of them, I am ashamed to say, until a few years ago when I began work (although I didn't know it at the time) on this book.

Since I have been a reporter on public affairs for most of my working life, I had thought I was reasonably well informed about what was happening in the United States. In the spring of 1967 I found I was wrong. At that time I was working—part-time and out of a reluctant sense of duty—as a member of one of the many commissions appointed by President Lyndon Johnson. This one was called the National Advisory Commission on Rural Poverty. Its chairman was Edward Breathitt, then governor of Kentucky—one of a string of able governors that state has elected in recent years. With the help of a small professional staff, the commission was supposed to find out why so many poor people kept moving from the countryside into the big cities, and what, if anything, could be done to stop this migration before the cities were swamped with more hungry, untrained, and hopeless migrants than they could possibly feed and house. (When the commission in due course submitted some answers, Mr. Johnson did not like them. He ignored its recommendations and tried with partial success to suppress its report.)

As the commission moved around the country, holding hearings and talking to hundreds of people—from governors to grape-pickers—I began to realize how much I had been missing. For one thing, I was surprised to find that in many places the old, familiar forms of government had simply broken down. Of course, everybody knew that the cities were in bad trouble. But I had not suspected that so many other instruments of government—states, counties, townships, supposedly powerful federal agencies—weren't functioning either.

As a consequence, big stretches of the country were lapsing into something close to anarchy. In these places, nobody —no mayor, governor, county commissioner, or anybody else—had the power to carry out even the elementary duties of government. Nobody had the authority, or money, to provide the local residents with a dependable supply of clean water, or a decent education, or a safe way to get rid of their garbage and sewage. If a citizen needed help in getting a roof over his head, or a job, or some attention from a doctor, or a quart of milk for a hungry baby—as millions did in 1967, and still do—he could find no one to talk to. He could find bureaucrats and officeholders aplenty, and some would listen with sympathy; but all too often they had to tell him that he had, indeed, come to the wrong place. And, sorry, they couldn't say where he ought to go.

These failures of government have never been adequately reported by the American press. Part of the fault, I have come to believe, lies with the universities. As Professor Stanley Scott of the University of California once remarked to me, the study of local government "hasn't been intellectually respectable in the academic community for the last thirty years." During the New Deal era, the political scientists focused their attention on Washington, where the action was. During World War II, and most of the time since, they have been preoccupied with international affairs. Moreover, during the thirties and forties several ambitious attempts to modernize state and metropolitan governments had failed; as a result, many professors decided that this was a discouraging and barren field of study. Now, of course, every alert university is hastily trying to organize a Center for Urban Studies, and having a hard time finding the people to staff it. But for at least a generation the universities turned out relatively few graduates who had an

educated interest in local government, much less the training to report it competently. Typically, therefore, newspaper
editors and writers have tended to cover such matters in a
perfunctory and tedious fashion. Besides they are accustomed to reporting "events": i.e., what happened at 3 P.M.
yesterday afternoon. When the structure of government
flakes away, it is likely to do so undramatically and over a
long period of time; therefore it isn't "news." And newspaper
publishers, who often are Chamber of Commerce boosters
and ad salesmen at heart, hate to admit that something is
going dreadfully wrong in their home communities.

Such at least was the explanation, or excuse, I offered for
my failure to grasp how far the collapse of government had
gone in this country, and what its consequences might be.
By 1968, when the commission's report was completed,
three of these consequences had struck me as especially
noteworthy.

One of them was a migration of epic proportions. During
the previous fifteen years, more than 10 million people had
moved from the countryside into the metropolises. A shift of
population on this scale makes the Goths' incursion into the
Roman Empire look like a Sunday outing—although the
results often have been remarkably similar. Inevitably it
caused bone-cracking disruptions, social, economic, and
spiritual. Half of the nation's three thousand counties lost
population, and hundreds of once-thriving crossroads communities faded into ghost towns, where the movie theater
and feedstore are boarded up and only a few old men are
left to doze in chairs tilted against the courthouse wall.
Those who left had been forced off the land by technological
changes which wiped out millions of jobs in agriculture; by
wrongheaded government farm programs, originally well-
intentioned; and by the failure of our society to provide any
other way for them to make a living. Most of them headed

for the big cities, in search of the jobs, housing, medical care, or welfare payments they needed to survive. Often they were disappointed, because many of the cities were nearly as close to impotence as the small towns and rural townships they had deserted. Nevertheless, 84 per cent of our population is now crowded into only 212 metropolitan areas; less than 5 per cent remains on farms. So long as this flow continues, the problems of the cities, from crime in the streets to threat of bankruptcy, probably are insoluble. Fortunately, the great migration now seems to be coming to an end—partly because America's farms are about as depopulated as they can be, short of abandonment to the buffalo; partly because several things are happening to halt and, in certain areas, even to reverse the stream.

An equally far-reaching effect of the failure of government, it seems to me, was a loss of confidence in American institutions. An incalculable number of people—especially among the young—abandoned faith in a system that obviously was not working very well. At home it apparently could find no way to cope effectively with poverty and the destruction of the environment; overseas it stumbled on with a war nobody wanted. Alienation comes naturally to any reasonably bright youngster who looks at Bedford-Stuyvesant or sniffs the waters of Lake Erie, or listens interminably to the Watergate scandals. After all, why should he be expected to love a country pocked with scenes so unlovable as Newark, Los Angeles, and the strip-mined hillsides of West Virginia?

Yet on second thought I began to suspect that such disillusionment, though understandable, might not be altogether justified. For the breakdown of the traditional structures of society was not the end of the story. The failure of government had a third consequence, perhaps the most significant of all: new institutions started to rise on the ground where the old ones had crumbled. As I traveled about the country on the work of the commission, I was astonished at the number of determined men and women I met who were trying to build a scaffolding of one sort or another for such institutions. Some of their designs looked timid and ineffectual, others more promising—but in nearly all cases these people were working in the dark, because they had not heard about similar experiments going on elsewhere. So it occurred to me that it might be useful to spread the news. I began to write a series of articles, most of which appeared in *Harper's Magazine*, about what Jim Ellis was doing in Seattle, and Ralph Widner in Appalachia, and Dan Sweat in Atlanta, and scores more in other places. Each article brought in letters about additional ventures in social reconstruction, in Oklahoma, in the Four Corners country, in my home state of Connecticut.

By 1972 I was wondering whether this—rather than Charles Reich's dreams of the counterculture—might be the real greening of America. For the pace of innovation had stepped up remarkably, not only in local communities but also (very quietly) in Washington, and in regions embracing several states. Patterns began to emerge. I found that I could sometimes guess in advance where Phil Hammer's invention would work, or under what circumstances Ted Kolderie's scheme might be more successful than J. J. Daniel's—and vice versa. Now and then I got the feeling that all of these inconspicuous changes could add up to the biggest transformation America has experienced since the Civil War.

Already our traditional federal system has changed into something George Washington would never recognize, although most of the old titles and political labels remain in place. That system was originally designed, in the simile of the late Morton Grodzins, to look like a layer cake. The national government was on top, the states were in the middle, and the cities and counties formed the base; each layer was supposed to have its own separate and carefully defined functions. Today the system looks more like a marble cake, with each layer swirled and mixed with every other. Dozens of federal agencies are deeply enmeshed in local government. States are trying to co-ordinate federal departments, which seldom can co-ordinate themselves. Moreover, the new institutions that are burgeoning all over the landscape cannot be accurately described as either local, state, or federal. When you look closely at any of them— whether a local development district or a multi-state region —you find it is a mixture of all three: a wondrous hybrid, unlike anything the Founding Fathers ever dreamed of.

To make the picture more perplexing, these new institutions have not yet found stable shapes. Through a process of trial and error, they are still evolving. The less successful probably will wither and die within the next few years, while the better ones grow stronger and more sharply defined. The most interesting questions about them cannot yet be answered. Will the best of these experiments knit together eventually to form a coherent whole—a new kind of federal system serving the entire nation? If the answer to that one turns out to be yes, will the new system get itself in working order early enough to cope with the immense physical and social changes the United States will be going through during the next quarter of a century?

Planning for a Second Nation

If General Electric expected to double its plant capacity and office space within the next twenty-five years, you can be sure it would assign a platoon of its ablest executives to figure out the best way to do it. In fact, General Electric almost certainly is doing that right now. I have talked to some of its planning officers, who were discreet (for obvious reasons) about their specific projects, but were candid enough about their operations in general. Their job is to answer questions about the future. When will a new factory be needed—for radios, refrigerators, or some entirely novel product? What should be its initial capacity and how much allowance should we make for expansion? How shall we raise the money? Where should we build it—taking into account the location of markets, labor supply, raw materials, rail and highway networks, the quality of local schools, and dozens of similar considerations? Such inquiries, for example, underlay the company's decision to build a $250-million manufacturing and distribution center at the new town of Columbia, Maryland; within ten years it is expected to employ twelve thousand people.

In such long-range planning, General Electric is not remarkable. It is simply following sound business practice. Every enterprise of any consequence has a professional staff at work on its plans for future growth. Every enterprise, that is, except the United States of America.

Within the next quarter of a century this country will need to double, roughly, its entire physical plant. This means that we face the job of building a second America— of duplicating all our man-made assets—within a single generation. What our forefathers did in three hundred years, we have to do again in less than a tenth of that time.

I wish this were not true. I'm a Zero Growth man myself, and it is obvious that we (and the rest of the world) will come to a No Growth policy eventually, simply because our planet and its resources are not expandable. But not yet. Within the decades just ahead, this country has little choice but to build as it never has before. This seems inescapable, for three reasons.

1. We have lagged a long way behind. For the last thirty years or so, we have spent the best of our resources and energies on wars, preparation for future wars, and the rebuilding of war-shattered nations in Europe and Asia. Meanwhile, we invested relatively little at home. We did not build enough new houses, for one thing, to replace those that wore out, much less to take care of a lot of new families. Our railroads fell apart. Our slums festered and erupted. Many of our factories became obsolete, so that they can no longer compete on even terms with their more up-to-date rivals in Japan, Germany, and even Korea. So if we hope to arrive someday at an Almost Good Society (or even to pay for our oil imports), we have a lot of catching up to do, and fast.

2. We have to provide for a great many more people— perhaps as many as 100 million—before the end of the century. In spite of the fact that the American birth rate has fallen recently (and maybe only temporarily) to the lowest level in history, our population will keep on growing for at least another seventy years. Even the lowest estimates of the demographers indicate that our population, which was about 203 million in 1970, will reach 251 million by the year

2000.* Every one of these new citizens will be clamoring for houses, schools, parking lots, bus lines, airports, and a thousand other things, including some place to earn a living.

Furthermore, many are going to want these things in places where nothing much exists today. Relatively little of the coming growth will be in the old core cities, such as New York and Chicago. In fact, the core cities are likely to shrink, for reasons to be noted in a moment. The fastest growth, now and in prospect, is in three places: the suburbs, the medium-sized cities, and the still fairly rural South and Southwest.

3. We are going to have to do a good deal of extra building to deal with our environmental crisis. Cleaning up the mess will require heavy investment in a variety of new structures: sewage treatment plants, pyrolytic incinerators to get rid of garbage, recycling depots, water purification plants, smokeless factories. Virtually all of these will demand a sharp increase in electric power for their operation. That in turn means building new power plants, running on

* Some readers may suspect a contradiction here; in fact, the preceding sentences are simply an example of how tricky population statistics can be. The country will have a stable reproduction rate if each couple has only slightly more than two children. ("Slightly more," because some children will die before they are old enough to have children of their own.) For practical purposes, the United States has achieved that level, and the chances seem fairly good that we may hold to it. But that does not mean an instant Zero Growth rate. The explanation is that we now have an abnormally large number of women of childbearing age. They sometimes are described as the second post-World War II baby boom, because they are the children of the unusually large crop of babies born in the few years after World War II. If each of them has only two children, therefore, our population will continue to grow at least for several decades; demographers in the Census Bureau estimate that it may take two or three generations before the recurring humps in our population level, originating after World War II, flatten out altogether, like receding ripples in a pond.

either coal or atomic energy. To supplement our fast-dwin-
dling petroleum reserves, we shall have to mine the coal and
oil shale deposits underlying the western prairies—and to do
that, we must build new towns to accommodate the miners
and new railways to move their products. Both to clean up
the air and to save scarce gasoline, we shall have to replace
at least partially that beloved but increasingly impractical
American artifact, the automobile, with new transit systems.
The list could go on for pages. . . .

You might think that a nation faced with these urgent
undertakings would have a national plan for accomplishing
them, just as General Electric does on its smaller scale. If
we were Russians, no doubt we would have; but our society
doesn't work that way. Nowhere in Washington will you find
anybody with formal responsibility for figuring out where
the next 100 million people are going to live, or how they
will get to work, or who will put roofs over their heads.
Neither the White House nor Congress has ever said: "Here
is our blueprint for the future. This is what we want
America to look like twenty-five years from now, and these
are the steps to reach that goal." Almost certainly, neither of
them ever will say anything of the kind.

But that does not mean that intelligent planning is impossible in this country—that we are doomed to stumble into
the next century in the myopic, heedless fashion that has
messed us up in the past. On the contrary, quite a lot of good
planning is going on right now—far more than ever before
in our history. It is not very visible, because it is being done
piecemeal, by many people and agencies, official and unofficial, all the way from Washington to Puget Sound. The
surprising thing is how often these bits and pieces add up, in
some mysterious fashion, to a fairly coherent blueprint for a
city, a region, or even the nation as a whole. Even more

surprising is the fact that such plans quite often get carried out.

For instance, something close to a plan for America's future growth already is in existence. It sets forth in broad outline a design for the second America: where our next 100 million citizens, and all the structures they will need, ought to be located, and how to get them there. It also suggests ways to accommodate the coming growth with a minimum of social and environmental damage. The goals proposed are clear, sensible, and well within the nation's capacity. (Provided, of course, that we avoid another war, a hopeful assumption that underlies everything in this book.)

The Growth Plan was produced by a curious, and uniquely American, process. It is contained in the reports of five commissions (although one of them called itself a committee), together with hundreds of pages of supporting data. These commissions worked independently of each other, but their ideas are remarkably similar. The recommendations of each one tend to complement and reinforce the recommendations of all the others. Nobody intended that their findings should thus fit together to form a comprehensive scheme of action—but it isn't altogether coincidence either. You might say that the pieces fell into that pattern because the spirit of the times demanded it; or, more prosaically, that when intelligent men stare long enough at the same body of facts, they are likely to arrive at similar conclusions.

Each of the five commissions was created as a political heat shield—a device for getting some planning done with a minimum of political risk. For until quite recently, planning was a risky business. Although it might be just dandy for businessmen, it was forbidden to politicians and civil servants. *Public* planning was regarded as a sin, indulged in by godless Communists but unthinkable for any right-minded

American. This dogma was proclaimed some forty years ago, when President Roosevelt tried to set up a National Resources Planning Board, on the theory that it might be useful to know what assets the nation had and how they were being used. The elderly conservatives who then dominated Congress promptly denounced the idea as subversive, cut off the Board's money, and drove some of its staff into political exile. This ruthless lesson was enough to make prudent bureaucrats shun the very word "planning" for decades to come.

Nevertheless, many people in government realized that some planning was necessary for the efficient conduct of the public business. Their problem was how to go about it without attracting the malevolent attention of congressional reactionaries. One solution—imperfect, but better than none —was to set up commissions.

Almost anybody can create one. Usually a commission is appointed by the President, but on occasion it may be organized by a cabinet member, a foundation, a congressional committee, or some convocation of mayors or governors. Its chairman is a more or less eminent citizen without political ambitions, and therefore not too nervous about criticism. His fellow commissioners ordinarily are obscure characters known as "experts," assorted to give at least token representation to blacks, women, labor, business, and any other pressure groups likely to be interested. Since it is a quasi-official body, it can be financed with tax money, or in a pinch by foundation grants—usually enough to hire a competent staff. Typically the commission is directed to study some question—almost always a politically sensitive one—and to come up with recommendations. If these turn out to be palatable, they can be adopted, with hosannas, by the original sponsor. If not, they can be repudiated or ignored.

Occasionally a commission produces immediate results, as in the case of the Hoover Commission which led in 1949 to a useful overhaul of the executive branch. More often a commission's findings will sound so radical, or expensive, that neither legislators nor executive agencies will dare touch them right away. Nevertheless the recommendations —and the thousands of pages of testimony and studies on which they are based—are now in the public domain. With luck, they will attract the attention of academics and maybe a few journalists; they will be referred to in books and congressional debates; and so their once startling propositions gradually become familiar. At that point they may be ripe for political action.

So it is with the five reports which comprise the Growth Plan. None of them has been officially adopted as public policy; two were disowned by the Presidents who commissioned them. Among the public at large, probably not one person in a thousand has read even one of them, much less all five. Yet they have attracted a fair amount of attention by the press and in learned journals; their main ideas are becoming familiar to public servants at all levels; they are used as texts in some graduate schools; and thus little by little their findings are becoming part of the political discourse.

Some of these findings are reflected throughout this book, but it may be useful at this point to indicate the main thrust of their argument. Each of the commissions concluded independently that our coming generations ought not to be crammed into our already overcrowded metropolitan areas. After all, it makes no sense to push 70 per cent of our people into 2 per cent of our land area. Yet government policies of long standing have had precisely that effect. Farm programs that originated with the New Deal, the welfare system, the rules for building public housing and insuring home mortgages, the location of government installations, the way public contracts are let—all these, and others, fostered the great postwar migration from the farms and small towns toward the big cities. To be sure, they were not intended to do so. Each of these policies was designed for a different, and usually well-meant, purpose. Only belatedly did it become apparent that they were, as an unanticipated by-product, influencing the direction of our national growth—and that the cumulative results were little short of disastrous.

How this happened is explained in two of the reports: one by the National Advisory Commission on Rural Poverty, the other by the Advisory Commission on Intergovernmental Relations. The first was a temporary, ad hoc group appointed by President Lyndon Johnson. He did not like its recommendations, partly because they criticized measures to which he was deeply committed (such as the subsidy of rich farmers at the expense of the poor), partly because he saw no way to finance them while the Vietnam war was going on. For months the report, entitled "The People Left Behind," lay buried in the White House and might never have been released if it had not leaked inadvertently to the press.

The Advisory Commission on Intergovernmental Relations is a permanent body, established in 1959 as a joint enterprise of federal, state, and local governments. Its main job is to scrutinize public policy at all levels, and to make recommendations for improvement. In its quiet way it has been doing some of the most hardheaded and farsighted planning ever undertaken in this country; the results are embodied in scores of reports, some of them highly technical. The most important of these (in my opinion at least) appeared in 1968 under the title "Urban and Rural America: Policies for Future Growth." It not only presents a reasoned criticism of government programs that have worked badly, or to unexpected ends, but also sets forth an array of alternatives. Some were adopted by the Nixon administration in its efforts to tidy up, or abolish, the innumerable programs inherited from earlier eras.

A third report, "Building the American City," is better known as the Douglas Report, after Paul H. Douglas, former senator from Illinois and chairman of the Commission on Urban Problems. It is the longest (more than five hundred pages) and offers the most detailed diagnosis of the cities' ills and the remedies necessary to cure them.

A companion document is "The New City," the product of the National Committee on Urban Growth Policy. Of all the five reports, it is the most accessible to the average reader, because it was brought out in an attractive format with plenty of pictures by a commercial publisher, Praeger ($12.50). Moreover it was edited by a professional writer-editor, Donald Canty. The other reports were published by the Government Printing Office in its usual drab style, and for the most part are written in the Late American Mandarin dialect which is now standard with bureaucrats and social scientists.

The most recent of the five, "Population and the American Future," has a history curiously like that of the report on rural poverty. It too was commissioned by a President—in this case Nixon—who did not like what he got. When he named John D. Rockefeller III to head the Commission on Population Growth and the American Future, he presumably thought he was choosing a safe man who would never come up with politically dangerous ideas. What the Rockefeller commission actually recommended, however, sounded downright radical in the climate of Nixon's Washington. Its suggestions for liberalizing abortion, birth control, and sex education policies, for example, were anathema to the President's Catholic following. Other recommendations—to help minorities break out of their ghettos, to eliminate "current patterns of racial and economic segregation," and to limit the growth of overcrowded cities—were hardly more palatable. Nixon repudiated the finding on abortion; the rest of the report he studiously ignored.

In its own way, each of the commissions urged policies that would lessen the pressure of population on our biggest cities. The Rockefeller commission put its main emphasis on reducing the number of births and enabling ghetto-dwellers to seek better jobs and living conditions elsewhere. The rural poverty report stressed measures to stem migration from the countryside to the metropolis and to encourage the growth of smaller towns in the hinterland. (Many a shabby and discouraged community of, say, 5,000 people can be converted into a thriving and attractive city of 50,000 to 100,000 if the right steps are taken to bring in new industry.) "The New City" called for the building of eleven new communities within the next thirty years, to provide homes and jobs for 20 million people. Ten of them would be cities of at least one million; the rest would average about 100,000 each.

Note that these three strategies are mutually supporting. They are simply different approaches to the same objective, and all three can be pursued at the same time. They are also consistent with the Douglas Report and the policies for future growth set forth by the ACIR. The two latter reports, however, go considerably further in specifying the kind of planning, land use controls, and other measures needed to reach that goal.

When I first read these five reports, my reaction was skeptical. They did add up, in a loose fashion, to a sort of grand design for America's future. And, yes, I had to admit that the design seemed to make good sense; certainly I could think of no alternative that looked more promising. But the whole thing sounded too grandiose to be practical. How would the country ever pay for it? And how could it ever become politically acceptable?

As I prodded deeper into the assembled evidence, however, my skepticism began to erode. I ended up convinced that the plan not only is feasible, but that it probably will be achieved in large part before the end of the century. Some of it is being achieved right now—enough, at least, to give me a reasonable hope that my grandchildren will live in a country less crowded, cleaner, more manageable, and more enjoyable than the America of today.

History itself seems to be moving in that direction. At least some of the historical reasons for the concentration of so many people in big cities are no longer at work. Consider the simple matter of transport. Throughout the ages, cities have grown up at those points where land and water routes meet. That was true of Corinth, Byzantium, London, and Delhi, to mention only a few of the great metropolises of the ancient world. It is equally true of New York, the natural place for transatlantic shipping to join the roads, waterways, and later railroads stretching into the interior of the continent. So too with Chicago, destined by geography to be the point where Great Lakes traffic met the transcontinental and southern rail networks. On a lesser scale, St. Louis burgeoned because it was the gateway to the West: the junction of the emigrant trails (and the railroads that followed) with the great waterways of the Mississippi and Missouri.

Today this kind of geographic advantage has been largely eclipsed, thanks to the internal-combustion engine. A manufacturer no longer has to locate his plants where they are well served by both rail and water. This is especially true of the new high-technology industries, which have no need to move large tonnages of ore and coal. They can build on any good truck route—such as Route 128 around Boston, the hive of the electronics industries. Even better is a site where several major highways come together near a good airport: say, Atlanta or Dallas.

Although Congress did not intend it that way, its vote after World War II to build a forty-thousand-mile network of interstate highways probably was the most important decision yet made concerning the future pattern of American growth. It is a prime cause of the dispersal of population now under way. Irrevocably it undermined the historic dominance of the old rail-and-water centers, and decreed a shift of industry to the hinterlands. As a consequence, nearly half of all the new manufacturing jobs opened up in the decade after 1960 were in *rural* areas, and many of the rest were in medium-sized cities, particularly in the South and West.

At the same time, the old core cities have been losing jobs—both to the new growth centers where interstate highways intersect, and to their own suburbs. New York City, for example, lost 73,300 jobs in 1971 alone, about 2 per cent of its total. Many of these have migrated to the suburbs, as the big corporations shifted their head offices as well as their manufacturing operations away from the urban core. According to the 1970 census, half of all the employment in our fifteen largest metropolitan areas was outside the boundaries of the mother cities. One incidental result was a sharp decline in commuting, that traditional bane of suburbanites. The great majority now work in the communities where they live; only a quarter of them still travel to core city jobs.

Another reason for the current shift of population is the very size of our biggest cities. They have bumped into something that the economists call "diseconomies of scale." In plain language this means that they are too expensive to run. After a city reaches a certain size—perhaps a million people—every additional increase in population means that each resident will have to pay more for everything. Not only for public services, such as water, garbage collection, police, and schools; *everything* will cost more, including food, the cost of moving around by taxi or bus, rent, parking spaces, and burglar insurance. That is why many nations consider New York City a "hardship post" and give extra pay to their diplomats who have to live there. It is also the reason why more companies decide each year that the cost of doing business there has become unbearable, so that it is time to look for a new location in some less congested place.

This is hard to demonstrate in precise figures, because our economists and political scientists have done surprisingly little work on the relationship between the size of cities and their cost of operation. We do have some fragmentary figures on governmental costs alone. In 1960, for example, cities under 150,000 population spent about $70 to serve each of their inhabitants, while cities above that size averaged about $123. But there is no evidence that the people in the bigger places got better schools, parks, sanitary services, or police protection. Quite probably they got worse.* Another significant comparison is that between New York and Chicago. New York has about twice as many people, but its budget at this writing is more than seven times as large. Nevertheless, Chicago has better schools—as measured by reading scores—better mass transit, and a better supply of reasonably priced housing.

---

* These facts, together with other evidence pointing in the same direction, were cited by Dr. Robert A. Dahl of Yale University in his presidential address to the American Political Science Association in Chicago, September 7, 1967. That speech, entitled "The City in the Future of Democracy," became famous in the trade because it raised so many previously ignored questions about the size of cities and the kind of population distribution that might be best for America. Another relevant discussion of the diseconomies of scale is included in the ACIR report on "Urban and Rural America: Policies for Future Growth."

Common observation is enough to show us why the biggest cities are so costly to run. Small communities typically get their water from a municipal reservoir close at hand. But New York has to reach out to the headwaters of the Delaware River 150 miles away and bring its waters into Manhattan through an expensive complex of tunnels, reservoirs, and pumping stations. To move its people, it has had to build—and is still building—a subway system fantastically costly both to construct and to operate. Such a dense concentration of humanity creates monumental problems of sewage and garbage disposal. The same density runs up the cost of crime and policing, as Oscar Newman has demonstrated in his *Defensible Space,* one of the most seminal books on architecture and town planning to appear in many years. He shows why crime goes up in direct relationship to the height of buildings and the number of their occupants. The typical high-rise apartments and public housing projects of the core city are, in fact, standing invitations to robbery, vandalism, and rape. Yet the cost of land makes it all but impossible to build anything else on an island as crowded as Manhattan.

The psychic costs of overcrowding are just as real as the economic ones. In recent years psychiatrists and anthropologists* have accumulated considerable evidence that both human beings and animals need a certain amount of elbow room for healthy development. When deprived of it, they are prone to aberrant behavior, including violence, homosexuality, abuse of their young, and mental illness. The political costs may be even greater, though harder to measure. In a city as large as New York the individual citizen inevitably feels remote from its governors, frustrated by its labyrinthine bureaucracy, and all but helpless to affect the decisions that mold his life. In such a setting a humane and

* Notably Dr. Kurt Richter of Johns Hopkins, Dr. Augustus F. Kinzel of Columbia's College of Physicians and Surgeons, and Dr. Edward T. Hall of the Illinois Institute of Technology.

responsive democracy simply is not feasible, for reasons noted from Plato through Jefferson to Robert Dahl. The latter's *After the Revolution?* (Yale University Press) is the best analysis I know of the fragile conditions under which a democratic system can work.

The best size for a happy community is a question that has been debated for two thousand years—though not nearly as much, in recent decades, as the subject deserves. Plato thought that the ideal number of citizens was 5,040 (not counting slaves and women, of course). Every citizen would then have a chance either to know one of the governing archons personally, or to know someone else who did; and that number, he believed, would be enough for "war or peace, for all contracts and dealings, including taxes and divisions of the land." Dahl has concluded that "the all-round optimum size for a contemporary American city is probably somewhere between 50,000 and 200,000." From my own empirical observations, I am inclined to agree; although I think it possible to stretch both upper and lower limits considerably, with tolerable if not optimum results. I am more than content with the town where I now live, with a population of about 13,000; yet I realize that if it were much smaller, it would be hard put to provide decent public services. At the other extreme, I am persuaded that cities as large as a million can be reasonably livable, if their population density is not too great and if they devise appropriate frameworks of government. (A few actually have.)

Recent public opinion polls apparently confirm the Dahl estimates. They indicate that most Americans would prefer, if they could, to live on farms or in small towns and suburbs, rather than in a big city. Fortunately an increasing number of them are now able to act on their desires. After the forced migration from countryside to city in the post-World War II decades, the demographic current has at last set the other way. So public preferences, tentative public policy—as outlined in the five reports mentioned earlier—and the tide of history all seem to foreshadow a spreading out of population, and an increasingly significant role for the small and medium-sized communities. It is there, if anywhere, that we may hope to find the Almost Good Society.

Most of this book, therefore, is concerned with what is happening in such communities. According to their size, circumstances, and history, they are developing different strategies for planning their future, and an assortment of new institutions to carry out these plans. The following chapters report on three types of strategies that strike me as particularly significant: one for small semi-rural communities, another for medium-sized cities, and a third for fairly large metropolitan areas. (But not for the largest. None of the institutions budding elsewhere in the country seem adaptable to a metropolitan area such as New York, which engulfs parts of three states.) In still later chapters we shall see how these local innovations might fit into the planning now under way for larger regions, embracing several states, and into some kind of overall national pattern, such as that suggested in the reports of the five commissions.

Unlikely as it may sound, the backcountry of Georgia is a good place to see what small, semi-rural communities can do to shape their future growth.

3.

The Georgia Invention

During the years of the Great Depression I got to know Georgia pretty well, because I then worked for a government agency that was trying to do something for sharecroppers, farm tenants, and other poor people in the rural South. I found it the most discouraged, and discouraging, state I had ever seen.

Our agency, the Farm Security Administration, made pitifully slow headway in Georgia because we had to fight every inch against a reactionary and apparently invincible political machine. Its boss was Ol' Gene Talmadge, a foulmouthed, gallus-popping redneck, whose avowed aims as governor were to keep the blacks in their place and the New Dealers out of the state. Behind him stood the plantation owners, the Klan, such big business as the state had, and the more bigoted and ignorant of the poor whites. Aside from naked violence, their chief weapons were the poll tax and a unique gimmick known as "the county unit system." These two devices in effect disenfranchised not only the poor and the black but also the residents of Atlanta, some of whom were suspected of moderate thoughts.

Under these circumstances any revolt against the power structure seemed hopeless; and until it was overthrown, progress of any kind seemed almost unimaginable. I made a last visit to Georgia with President Roosevelt shortly before

World War II, and came away so disheartened that I never wanted to see it again.

For more than thirty years I did not. But friends down there kept sending me reports that the times they were a-changin'. The poll tax and county unit system were gone. The old power structure had broken up. Thanks to the Supreme Court's one-man-one-vote ruling, democracy was creeping in. So were businessmen of a new stamp, who couldn't see any profit in keeping poor people poor. Atlanta was becoming a boom town, the de facto capital of the entire Southeast. It had acquired a black majority, a black mayor, a black head of the school system, several black millionaires, and the most self-confident black middle class of any American city.

For a long while I did not pay much attention to such tidings because I could not believe that anything really fundamental would change in Georgia during my lifetime. Then I began to get signals that the state not only was catching up with the rest of the nation but in some ways was actually pushing into the lead. It had, for example, come up with some political and social ideas of marked originality. Moreover, they had worked so well that they were beginning to spread to other states. So recently I decided that I had better go see for myself.

Everything I had heard turned out to be true, and then some.

For one thing, nobody had told me about the paint. In the old days I used to drive through the Cotton Belt for hours without seeing a sharecropper's cabin that had ever been graced with a lick of it. Dr. Will Alexander, who spent his life trying to drag the South out of its slough of despond, once remarked, "If I could ask the Lord for just one miracle, I would ask him to rain paint on Georgia." Somehow in the years of my absence that prayer evidently had been answered. An unpainted house in the countryside is now an exception rather than the rule, and most of the croppers' shanties have long since been torn down. The black families who once lived in them have moved to Atlanta or the big cities of the North—replaced by mechanical cotton pickers, chemical weed killers, and the new low-labor crops such as beef cattle and soybeans.

Neither was I prepared for the change in mood. The Georgians I talked to were no longer despondent, sullen, and suspicious. Typically they were ebullient and full of confidence. "Sure we've got problems, plenty of them," one Atlanta businessman told me. "But we've solved a lot worse during the last twenty years, and we know how to lick what's left. We have a lot of momentum going for us. We know that Atlanta is a city of the future, just as New York is a city of the past."

Of the many reasons for the awakening of Georgia and the rest of the South the most obvious is a massive injection of federal money. Political scientists never have a good word to say for the seniority system in Congress, but Southerners don't complain about it. When one of their men gets to Congress, they have traditionally kept on electing him practically for life. The recent growth of the Republican Party in the South may change this cozy arrangement, but for generations seniority automatically put Southerners in control of nearly all the key congressional committees, with their hands on the money spigots. Consequently for the last forty years the South has enjoyed much more than its proportionate share of federal spending—for economic development, highways, military installations, schools, and a broad array of other aid programs. And fair enough. From the Civil War until the New Deal (when the lush, green stream began to flow out of the Treasury) the South had been on short rations; since then it has felt entitled to its turn at the trough.

It is also true, however, that the southern states have

become remarkably adept in extracting money from Washington—not only through the blessings of congressional seniority—and spending it to generally good purpose. To do so, they had to create a new form of local government, an almost revolutionary undertaking in that tradition-bound part of the world. It originated in Georgia, and after a successful trial run there it was picked up by neighboring states. At this writing it has taken root in places as distant as New England and the Pacific Northwest; and within the next few years it seems likely to cover, in one form or another, virtually the whole country.

Although it goes by different names from state to state, this new arm of government was originally known as a "local planning and development district." (An intentionally innocuous title: who, in the underdeveloped South, could be against development?) It was invented and put on the political agenda by three men, none of whom had either money or any political clout to speak of: Philip Hammer, then a young city planner in Atlanta; J. W. Fanning, a vice-president of the University of Georgia; and—surprisingly— Frank Hood of the Georgia Power Company.

For decades Georgia Power had been one of the big mules, in the local phrase, of the old, conservative ruling clique. Consequently it took Hood a long while to persuade the few liberals in the state that a political idea he was sponsoring could be really progessive. In fact, some of the company's top executives were, initially, deeply suspicious about what he was up to, but Hood's argument for his pet reform was so persuasive that he finally brought them around.

Hood's job in the mid-fifties was industrial development. He was supposed to lure new industries into the state, with the expectation that they would become good customers of Georgia Power. This was a tough assignment, because much of Georgia—especially its rural areas, which needed jobs most desperately—was not attractive to modern industry.

For one thing, most of the countryside had no effective government. In the dim Colonial past Georgia had been divided into 159 counties, nearly all of them too small, too poor, and too incompetent to deliver anything except a naked minimum of governmental service. Often the county courthouse sheltered a judge, a sheriff, and a tax collector, and that was about it. Nobody knew how to apply for a federal grant. Nobody even knew what federal money might be available for the county, much less which bureaus handed it out.

Every county was competing with every other for new industries, but all were hopelessly inept competitors. In approaching a northern textile company, for instance, the local officials could mumble something about "plenty of cheap labor" and maybe offer a tax-free building site. But they rarely could say how much labor actually was there, because they had no reliable statistics. They had to admit that many workers were barely literate because the school system was no good. No money was in sight for vocational training. Neither were there any solid facts on such elemental matters as water supply, markets, natural resources, and population trends. Consequently a rural community— even with Hood's volunteer help—seldom could make a convincing pitch.

The obvious remedy for this sorry plight was to abolish nine tenths of the counties in Georgia and replace them with new units of government large enough to operate efficiently. But because of local chauvinism and the ferocious opposition of local officeholders, this prescription was not politically feasible.

Could a way be found, then, to accomplish much the same thing by indirection?

Phil Hammer thought so. His planning duties had made him achingly familiar with the problem, and he had been discussing it for some time with a fellow spirit—J. W.

Fanning, who was then working on schemes for community development at the state university. By the mid-fifties they had evolved an idea that seemed both workable and politically acceptable, and they took it to Hood, who looked like a natural ally.

In essence, they proposed to coax a dozen or so neighboring counties to band together into something that might be called a "planning and development district." No county boundary would be disturbed. No officeholder need feel that his job was threatened. But by pooling their efforts and what little money they had, the confederated counties could afford to hire at least one professional to make a study of the economic assets and possibilities of the whole district. Armed with this data, he could then make a systematic search for those industries that could best use the available assets; and this time, it was hoped, his sales talk would prove more enticing.

Hood bought the idea with enthusiasm, since he had been thinking along similar lines. Better yet, he offered to put up some Georgia Power money for the preliminary missionary work—not much, but enough to pay for the expenses of the three evangelists as they traveled up and down the state, preaching the glorious possibilities of planning and development districts to every Rotary Club, Chamber of Commerce, and sewing circle they could get to listen.

After five years on the road, they finally stirred up enough interest to make the legislature pay serious attention. In 1960 it passed a law authorizing any combination of counties to organize themselves into a development district; and before the year was out, eleven counties in the Coosa Valley did just that. No monument has yet been put up to commemorate this historic event—the birth of the nation's first development district—but someday it may come.

Today all of Georgia's 159 counties have voluntarily clumped themselves together into eighteen development districts. The state university, under Fanning's leadership, and the state planning agency suggested logical groupings, based on geographic, political, and economic factors, but these were not imposed on local officialdom. Each county could decide for itself which neighboring counties—if any—it wanted to work with. From the beginning, therefore, the districts were regarded as local creations, rather than a new-fangled notion imposed by the state.

Their functions have grown far beyond their original modest purpose of enticing new industries. In many cases they have become full-fledged instruments of government, doing a wide array of jobs that individual counties could never have dreamed of tackling. Perhaps the most important of these is the protection of the environment—so often in the past thoughtlessly sacrificed to any new development, from a strip mine to a paper mill.

One of the most successful districts, of the many I have visited, is located in the mountain country of northeastern Georgia. Long ago I had known it as one of the most woebegone backwaters of the South. The people there are mostly poor whites, about 200,000 of them, scattered thinly among the green coves and hollows. For generations they had scraped out a living—more meager year by year—by lumbering, hunting, moonshining, and sporadic work in a few textile mills. Nor did they have much hope of anything better, because most of the land is too steep for farming and it yields no coal or other minerals.

Things began to look up about 1962 when thirteen counties joined to form the Georgia Mountains Planning and Development District, with Oliver Terryberry, a specialist in farm management, as its first executive director. Its first years were spent mainly in gathering information; the district had never even been properly mapped, and useful statistics were almost nonexistent. Not until 1965 was the new organization geared up for effective operations—and, by happy coincidence, at just that time it got a strong boost from Washington.

Lyndon Johnson had declared his War on Poverty. A number of federal agencies—notably the Appalachian Regional Commission and the Economic Development Administration—were offering to ladle out money to conspicuously hungry areas such as this. But there were strings attached. Some people in Washington had noted what was going on in the Coosa Valley and a few other pioneer development districts, and it had occurred to them that such institutions could serve as a handy conduit for government grants. For each district had at least a rudimentary plan for building up the local economy; it knew what things were needed, in what order of priority, and how much they would cost. It had some capability, therefore, to parcel out the money in an orderly and coherent fashion—which was more than you could say for the individual counties or, for that matter, most state governments. So the word went out from Washington: "Shape up into development districts, if you want to get your share of the loot." As a further incentive, Washington offered to put up most of the cash to pay for a staff of professional planners wherever such a district was organized. In effect the federal government had picked up the idea born so modestly in the Coosa Valley and had decided to try to apply it nationwide.*

A district such as the Georgia mountains that already had a staff at work obviously was off to a long head start. When I visited it, the day-to-day operations were in the hands of Sam Dayton, a lean, intense young man who had taken over the directorship when Terryberry retired a year earlier. He is a Ph.D. in economic geography who came to the job with unlimited enthusiasm; eight years of prior experience in

* Why and how this happened is a complicated story, recounted in detail by James L. Sundquist in his *Making Federalism Work*, published in 1969 by the Brookings Institution.

local planning, military service, and the federal bureaucracy; and an intimate knowledge of the area. He was born
and raised in Gainesville, its main town (about eighteen
thousand people), and had served as chief planner under
Terryberry before taking over the top job.

I met him in the cramped, starkly functional little cinder-
block building near the Gainesville railroad tracks that
houses the district headquarters. There Dayton supervises
twenty-eight planners and development specialists, all
trained professionals. (I had expected that at least some of
them would be patronage appointees and political hacks, in
the venerable Georgia tradition; I was mistaken.) They are
something of a curiosity in that part of the country, since
before their coming the entire district could muster only five
public employees with professional expertise: three city
managers, a county manager, and a single town planner.

One thing in which Dayton and his staff are expert is, as
the local politicians put it, "milking the feds." They know
what grants and loans can be extracted from dozens of
federal agencies, for what purposes, under what conditions
—and how to unsnarl the miles of red tape necessary to get
them: in itself an arcane art. Thus they have been able to
help their thirteen counties and thirty-nine municipalities to
file and push through applications for scores of projects—
water and sewer systems, roads, health clinics, vocational
schools, parks, police communications equipment, libraries,
and the like. By 1971 more than $20 million in federal
money had been siphoned into the district as a direct result
of such wangling.

All of these things, be it noted, are necessities for a reasonably civilized life; the mountain people had wanted them
for years but could never afford them on their own. The
same things are necessary to attract industry and create
jobs, since no company wants to move into an area without
decent hospitals, schools, roads, and water supply. They are

the first prerequisite—the "infrastructure," as the planners say—for lasting economic development.

They paid off quickly. By 1971 the district had acquired a plastics factory, a plant building alternators for Chrysler cars, a four-hundred-job factory for making prefabricated houses, plus a variety of metal- and wood-working firms.

"We are choosy now," Dayton told me. "We are past the time when we were glad to take in any firm that would promise a few jobs. For example, we are now discouraging industries that would pollute the air or streams, or put a lot of heavy trucks on our mountain roads. We have come to realize that our most valuable assets up here are the scenery, lakes, and rivers, and we are not about to let them be ruined."

These assets he sees as the basis of a thriving recreation industry—including, of all things, a ski resort already open for business. (It gets only five inches of natural snow a year, but artificial snow extends the season to almost ninety days. Customers are no problem. Would you believe that Atlanta, a two-hour drive to the south, has the nation's biggest ski club?) Summer resorts, fishing camps, tourist attractions, and motels also are being encouraged, and sometimes financed, through the development district.

What made a resort industry practicable was another federal investment: a superhighway that brought the once all but inaccessible mountains within commuting range of Atlanta. It also brought hazards. Lake Lanier and a half a dozen lesser lakes in the mountain valleys might easily have been turned into eyesores by the kind of shore development—sleazy cabins, filling stations, marinas, and eateries—that has desecrated so many waterfronts in New England and the Middle West. To stave this off, Dayton and his staff are promoting countywide zoning, a rarity in most of America. Two counties had adopted zoning rules to protect their lakes at the time of my visit, two more had them in the works, and Dayton was reasonably confident that within a few years the whole district will have its scenic resources safely guarded.

But not locked up. To get the best economic return out of Lake Lanier without ecological damage, Dayton's staff is pushing a carefully planned development on a cluster of islands. The Army Engineers provided access by means of a $400,000 causeway (courtesy of the late Senator Richard B. Russell, to whom the military rarely said no). Private investors are well started on a complex of hotels, summer homes, campsites, and marinas, together with advanced sewage treatment facilities, at a total cost of roughly $56 million—the largest single undertaking the Georgia mountains have ever known.

The most imaginative project I came across was a Shakespeare festival, the only one south of New York City. The National Shakespeare Company, which spends the school year touring college campuses, has been persuaded to spend its summers performing at Young Harris College, near the northern edge of the state. It is expected to bring a stream of overnight visitors to a hitherto neglected tourist area: and Dayton has hopes of extending the season by establishing a music festival and perhaps a ski resort.

One reason why planning has had a bad name in this country is that so much of it has been ineffectual. Early planners—often failed architects or visionaries, or both—habitually covered their maps with monumental avenues, ideal parks, and utopian residential areas, with little regard for either political or financial realities. Usually, therefore, their magnificent designs ended up in some forgotten closet in the basement of City Hall.

The planning going on in the Georgia mountains, and in most of the other development districts I know about, is something else. It works, because it is tightly linked to both the political and budgeting processes. Dayton and his staff are responsible to a board of twenty-nine commissioners, mostly elected officials, who represent each county and important town in the district—men attuned to the political heartbeat of their communities. They meet frequently to review the work of the staff and to discuss future projects. In addition, Dayton and his chief assistants spend much of their time traveling around the district, finding out what each community needs (and is willing to pay for, at least in part), and explaining how his proposals will affect local lives and bank accounts. So far the operation seems to be meeting with general public approval—although the setup does have some political weaknesses, potentially serious, to be noted a little later.

Every item that goes into the district plan also goes into a budget. Nothing is proposed until the commissioners know precisely how it will be paid for—how much from local taxes, how much from federal and state contributions, how much from private investors. There are, in fact, two plans. One is on a biennial basis, and is in an almost continual process of revision and updating. The other is a Comprehensive Development Plan, setting priorities over a six-year period; it includes a budget for all public spending, not only by the district but by all the fifty-two counties and municipalities within its borders.

High on the priority list is a housing authority, scheduled to build 1,500 homes the first year, largely financed through a variety of federal programs. (Half of the houses in the district are substandard.) Significantly, the authority will be managed by the district commission through Dayton's office —a long step beyond planning and into direct governmental operations. Similarly, the district plans to set up a Small Business Investment Corporation, and to develop a health scheme to provide clinics, hospitals, and ambulance service wherever needed. (One of the counties, Dawson, did not have a single doctor at the time of my visit, and throughout the district the majority of residents have never had really adequate medical and dental services.)

"Well," I remarked to Dayton, "all this sounds promising for the future. But is there any simple way to tell what the district actually has accomplished so far?"

He produced two tables of statistics. One showed that the number of people employed in the district had risen from 58,000 to 69,000 (in round figures) within the last five years. The other indicated that over a ten-year period the total of personal incomes had considerably more than doubled.

These figures have substantial meaning—for New York, Chicago, Cleveland, and Newark, as well as for the district itself. The chief export of the Georgia mountains, for generations, had been poor people traveling north in search of jobs. Because they typically were ill-educated and unskilled they often ended up on the relief rolls of some big city. Here—and in other poverty-breeding places throughout Appalachia, the old Cotton Belt, Puerto Rico, and elsewhere—is where the urban crisis came from. But by the early seventies the tide of migration from these mountain counties not only had halted, but had begun to flow the other way. That fact alone would seem to justify the investment American taxpayers have made in Sam Dayton's district.

It is also true—or so I believe—that the very existence of the Georgia Mountains Planning and Development District was responsible for bringing in much of that investment, and for putting it to productive use. Until its people created a governmental mechanism that operated effectively, nothing much could possibly happen for the better in those despairing valleys.

4.

A New Pattern for Rural America

I have described Sam Dayton's little kingdom in some detail because development districts (under whatever name) seem destined to become basic components in the new pattern of federalism that is now taking shape. By 1973 about six hundred of them had been set up in forty-nine states. In some places they are called Councils of Government, in others they are known as regional planning commissions, economic development districts, planning boards, regional councils, and other variants. (The nomenclature is confusing, so for the sake of simplicity I shall refer to all of them as development districts.) Within their boundaries they contain nearly 90 per cent of the country's population and 65 per cent of its land area.

It would be misleading to suggest that the Georgia mountains district is typical. It is more successful than most districts in Georgia, and all eighteen of the Georgia districts are ahead of most of their counterparts in other states. In fact, there is no such animal as a "typical" district, for they vary considerably in size, structure, and competence. Some have brought about important changes in the way people live and govern themselves, others have been almost completely ineffectual. Moreover, the districts operating in rural areas, such as Dayton's, are fundamentally different from those in metropolitan areas. But they all have certain characteristics in common:

1. They are peculiar hybrids, hard to fit into our traditional political theory. Are they arms of local government, or of the state, or of the federal government? The answer has to be: "A little of each."

They look like something local, because on the average they contain four counties and from fifteen to twenty municipalities, and their predominant concern is the guidance and development of these localities. Besides, the staff—on the average about eight professional planners and four clerical helpers—is responsible directly to a commission or council, which oversees the staff's work, approves its budget, and hires the director (and if necessary fires him). In some cases the council's members are all elected officials, usually the mayor of each town in the district and a county commissioner or judge from each county. In other cases, the elected officials appoint additional members—prominent citizens with the time and inclination for public service—to help carry the work load.

Yet the district's operating budget—typically about $250,000 a year—comes largely from the federal purse. In Dayton's case, roughly one fifth of his money comes from local levies, another fifth from the state, and all the rest from five different agencies in Washington. The proportions vary from one place to another, but virtually all districts depend on Washington for at least half of their budgets. Does this make them federal agencies?

(Federal revenue sharing may change, and perhaps simplify, the channels through which the money flows; but the proportion of federal funding is expected to remain substantial.)

If you look at the districts from another perspective, they seem to be creatures of the state. In most cases they are chartered by state legislation, and they report to a state agency—in Georgia, the Office of Regional Planning—

which may, or may not, try to fit their individual plans into an overall state development plan.

In practice, however, the development districts usually work much more closely with federal agencies than with anybody in the state capital.

2. For they are, in effect, the field troops for much of the federal bureaucracy. Washington agencies have been notoriously unable to co-ordinate their operations, because of bureaucratic jealousies and because Congress has given them confusing and often contradictory directives. What co-ordination there is has to be accomplished in the field by men like Sam Dayton. It is up to him to put together fragments of different federal programs—for roads, for housing, for water and sewers, for environmental protection, for airports and vocational schools—so they all dovetail together into a pattern that makes sense for his people. In addition, he is responsible for channeling big sums in federal loans and grants to the local authorities who will actually do the spending.

3. The districts derive most of their political muscle from the federal government. Its source is an extraordinary and little-known document labeled Circular A-95. I would gamble that not one reader in a hundred, aside from professional bureaucrats, has ever heard of it. Yet it is, for practical purposes, the Magna Carta of all the development districts in the country. It also, indirectly, is responsible for the existence of most of them. It would be nice to report that the Georgia Invention spread through beneficent contagion— that the development districts' success in their state of origin was so obvious that other states picked up the idea spontaneously. Alas, that is not the case. A few neighboring states—notably Tennessee and Kentucky—did follow the Georgia example on their own initiative; but the others moved only after a series of strong nudges from Washington, of which A-95 is the most recent and heaviest.

It was issued on February 9, 1971, by George P. Shultz, then director of the President's Office of Management and Budget, and was addressed to "the heads of executive departments and establishments." In free translation from Bureaucratic Mandarin, it orders them not to hand out any federal money to any city, county, or "organization or individual" unless the application has first been reviewed by the local development district.

Thus it confers on Sam Dayton, and his counterparts in some six hundred other districts, a fairly awesome power. In theory, he does not have authority to turn down the project. He is merely required to "comment" on the application, expressing agreement, disagreement, or suggestions for changing it. In practice, however, he exercises a veto. Almost never will a federal agency approve a request for money unless it is accompanied by a favorable "comment" by the director of the development district. And Sam is not supposed to approve unless the proposal fits into the district's overall development plan. Furthermore, he must certify that the project will do no serious harm to the environment.

What actually happens in most cases is something like this. Suppose the town of Dahlonega wants to ask the federal Department of Housing and Urban Development for half a million dollars to build a sewage system. If he is astute, the mayor will first discuss the idea informally with Sam. The professionals on Sam's staff will then check the proposal against the district's master plan. Is the site of the proposed sewage treatment plant in the right place—or will it be flooded when the Army Engineers build a dam a couple of years from now under another project already in the works? Would it be more economical to combine the Dahlonega system with another one needed by a neighboring town? Will the effluent from the treatment plant pollute a stream? Is the system big enough to take care of the prob-

able growth of the community after the Appalachian highway network is completed? Would it result in the destruction of any area of "unique natural beauty, historical, and
scientific interest"?

If the staff comes up with favorable answers to these and
dozens of similar questions, Dahlonega will then make out a
formal application (with the staff's help) and it will be sent
on to Washington with Sam's enthusiastic comment. If not,
Sam will tactfully explain his objections to the mayor and
the town council. Perhaps a better site might be found? Or
wouldn't it be wise to postpone the enterprise for a year,
when the proposed plant could be merged with a more
comprehensive sewage system to serve a larger area?
Chances are that the town fathers and the district staff will
work things out. Nobody wants to send an application to
Washington with an unfavorable comment.

Weakly run districts, and those which have not yet
worked up a master plan, sometimes send along all requests
for money with a favorable comment, after only a perfunctory "review." I have met some district directors who hate
the whole A-95 procedure because they are afraid to say
no—however tactfully and tentatively—to an elected politician. Occasionally such goof-off districts are spotted by
someone in Washington, and their project applications are
returned "for further study." Sad to say, however, it is possible for a district staff to get away with such sloppy work
for a long time. Nobody in Washington or in most state
capitals is now organized to subject the local districts to
systematic scrutiny, much less discipline.

For projects involving metropolitan areas or more than
one district, the "clearinghouse function"—as the A-95 review process is often called—is delegated to other planning
authorities of appropriate scope. In the case of Atlanta, for
instance, the job is handled by the Atlanta Regional Commission, created in 1971 to guide the future growth of the

whole metropolis, now spreading over five counties. For statewide undertakings, the responsibility normally rests with the state planning agency.

In earlier years, individual federal agencies—notably the Appalachian Regional Commission and the Economic Development Administration—had insisted that their projects be cleared through the local development districts. Moreover, as early as 1966 the Demonstration Cities and Metropolitan Development Act had required all applications from big cities to be reviewed by some kind of comprehensive planning agency for the whole metropolitan area.* But A-95 was the first order from the White House that authorized the districts to review and co-ordinate a wide range of federal undertakings: specifically, 145 listed programs, administered by more than a score of agencies ranging from the Department of Agriculture to the Army Engineers. Since nearly all development projects now involve some federal money, this directive gives Sam Dayton and his counterparts the power that earlier planners had generally lacked: the means to see that their plans actually are carried out.

Nearly all of the district directors I have met quite evidently enjoy their work. Typically they are young men, because planning has become a youthful profession. Until the sixties there were not a great many jobs in this field, and most of them were in the big cities. What openings there were rarely seemed attractive to the young and adventurous, because the work of city planners was so often ignored or

---

* Thanks largely to the efforts of Senator Muskie. Much of the credit for the whole idea of local review also belongs to the Advisory Commission on Intergovernmental Relations. One of its main jobs is to find ways to make the different levels of government mesh, rather than clash. It fathered the Intergovernmental Co-operation Act of 1968, which provides the legal basis for Circular A-95. Much of the groundwork was laid by two unusually able and dedicated public servants: William G. Colman, then executive director of the commission, and his assistant, David B. Walker.

compromised by the politicians who actually ran things. All
that changed when Washington began to demand plans—
"comprehensive" and "workable," as they were usually described—from every community that wanted federal money.
Suddenly there were more planning jobs, all over the country, than there were experienced planners. They had to be
filled largely by men recently graduated by university planning departments (and there weren't many good ones) or
young men who had a year or two of on-the-job training
with land development firms. Salaries were bid up fast.
Today top planners are among the best-paid public servants,
often earning more than small-town lawyers or businessmen. Probably more important, the nature of the profession
changed. Planners no longer had to work in a power vacuum; thanks to Circular A-95 (and earlier Washington
directives in the same vein) they could at last make things
happen. They had a chance to become operators, rather
than visionaries.

Sam Dayton is a case in point. He is overworked and a
little tense, but he knows he is accomplishing something
important for communities he loves. He can see the results
every day. And though I think he has less vanity than most
of us, I suspect he can't help but be aware that in a few
short years he has become a big man in northeast Georgia,
known and respected by people of consequence.

An equally engaging example is Donald R. Hinson, who
runs the South Carolina Appalachian Council of Governments. Only thirty-four years old when I first met him, he
wears sideburns and mod clothes and has the build of a
military policeman, which he once was. His suite of offices
in Greenville, South Carolina—spacious, carpeted wall to
wall, and furnished with modern furniture and abstract
paintings—would do credit to Madison Avenue. (This carries a certain symbolic significance because many public
employees throughout the South still work in some dingy

corner of a courthouse, with splintered chairs and smelling of disinfectant.)

Like most men in his kind of position, Hinson is not a political appointee. In fact, he is not even a native of the state; he was born in North Carolina and trained in its universities as a planner and civil engineer. He gave up a promising career with a private land development firm to take his present job—partly because he is interested, like so many young people these days, in doing something socially useful, partly because he finds the work exciting. After all, not many men of his age have the chance to run an enterprise that already has handled $59 million in federal funds alone and that has responsibility for shaping the future of more than a half million people.

He talks about that future with infectious enthusiasm. Until recently Greenville was a shabby, somber little textile city not markedly different from a dozen others strung along the Appalachian Piedmont, between the mountains and the coastal plain. Now it is a boom town, crackling with the kind of excitement I remember when I was growing up in north Texas during the glory years of the big oil strikes. A decade of tedious, slogging economic development work—largely backed with federal money—has at last pushed Greenville to the takeoff point.

From low-wage cotton cloth manufacturing, it has gradually branched into the better-paying lines of textile machinery, synthetic fibers, dyestuffs, and related chemicals. German investment and technology are flowing into the region, along with a good many millions from big American firms. Energy for the new plants comes from a $300-million hydroelectric and nuclear power complex. A plentiful supply of water is guaranteed by the Hartwell Dam; and as a by-product a lucrative recreation business is developing along the reservoir's 963 miles of shoreline—campgrounds and boat-launching ramps furnished by the Army Engineers.

Still other tourist opportunities are being opened up by federal highway projects, notably the Cherokee Foothills Scenic Route. (Much of the money for these undertakings comes from the Appalachian Regional Commission, another creative innovation in government, as we shall see in later pages.)

Hinson is confident that Greenville, and the forty-two other towns within his domain, can avoid the mistakes of the older industrial centers in the North. By careful advance planning, he hopes, they can scatter the new factories throughout the six counties, at sites that not only make economic sense, but also will forestall the congestion and blight of, for example, the old New England mill towns. Already some of his communities are joining together to build sophisticated sewage treatment systems—not to rescue polluted streams, but to make sure ahead of time that they never will be polluted. And so on, for the planning of health facilities, housing, recreation areas, and a score of other interlacing projects.

What Hinson seemed proudest of are the district's schools. Though it lacks a major university, the district is building what, at this stage, it needs even more: a top-notch network of vocational and technical schools. Nine vocational schools are in operation, turning out some 1,600 trained graduates every year; two more are under construction. In addition, three technical-education centers now enroll 9,600 students of all ages. One of them may be the best in the country for training paramedical people, from laboratory technicians to dentists' assistants. Others work closely with local industries. When a new factory goes up, its manager can arrange in advance to have the right number of people trained for each kind of job—and the students are assured that jobs will be waiting when they finish the course. For young people who had, until recently, little hope for anything except sharecropping or waiting tables, these opportunities are pretty heady.

Here, as in the Georgia mountains, the tide of migration has been reversed. The number of people holding jobs in the six Appalachian counties of South Carolina went up by 11 per cent in the four years after Hinson's program got going in 1967, and their average incomes nearly doubled.

It is no coincidence that race relations in the district have improved very considerably. Greenville used to be a stronghold of the Klan, and so long as poor whites and poor blacks had to compete for scarce jobs, animosities were inevitable. Today they are far less evident. The Greenville schools were integrated with no fuss, and many better-paying jobs—once tacitly reserved for whites—are increasingly being filled by blacks. The three black professionals on Hinson's staff work on excellent terms, so far as I could discern, with their twenty-two white colleagues.

Good as it is, this record is not unique. Indeed, Greenville is merely the southeastern corner of something that might be called the Growth Quadrangle—an area roughly bounded by invisible lines stretching to three other corners: Oak Ridge, Tennessee (where the atoms came from); Kingsport, Tennessee; and a still unnamed metropolis in North Carolina where Raleigh, Durham, and Chapel Hill are coalescing into a single community. For investors and for ambitious young people looking for action, it is an interesting place to watch.

The action can take many forms. Walter J. Brown found it by becoming the country's first circuit-riding city manager.

Most of the towns in the Piedmont are too small, and still too poor, to afford much in the way of professional staff. The village of Duncan, South Carolina, has only two employees: a full-time policeman and a clerk who works ten days a month. Many others are run, in a fashion, by their mayors and councilmen—typically small merchants, realtors, or lawyers with no governmental experience, who try to take care of the civic business in their spare time.

To help them out, Hinson's office hired Brown, a professional city manager with sixteen years' experience. He travels around the district, visiting every town that needs his expertise—in one place to draft the first municipal budget it has ever had, in another to draw up a personnel manual or a dog-control ordinance. He has uncovered long-overlooked state laws providing for phone and electric service for places that had never had them. Elsewhere he is helping mayors apply for federal money to build a park or buy a patrol car. Obviously he is having a lot of fun.

In all that I have said about development districts so far, I may have given the impression that I regard them as the greatest invention since the umbrella, which they much resemble. That is only half correct. The districts are so new and so spotty in their performance that it is not yet possible to draw up anything but a highly tentative balance sheet. Already, however, it is clear that they have serious weaknesses as well as strengths. My own hesitant conclusions, plus and minus, after some five years of study and observation run like this:

Minus

1. *They have all the structural faults of the Southern Confederacy and of the original thirteen states under the Articles of Confederation.*

That is, they are purely voluntary organizations. Any member county or municipality can pick up its marbles and leave anytime it chooses. By so doing, it might give up a lot of federal money since it would no longer have a voice in the A-95 clearinghouse process—but in some cases when a locality felt strongly that the district plan would work to its disadvantage, it has done just that.

Moreover, the governing board of a district normally reaches its decisions only by unanimous consent. Any member—even the smallest town—can veto a project or the whole district plan if it doesn't like it. In a few instances the governing boards act by majority vote; Hinson told me that this is now the practice in his South Carolina Appalachian Council of Governments. But again this is merely a voluntary arrangement, which could be upset whenever a single member wants to force the issue. Consequently Hinson, who is no dummy, tries to make sure that no really tough, divisive question ever comes before the board.

Worse yet, development districts lack nearly all of the powers of true government. They cannot tax. Consequently they are totally dependent on voluntary contributions from their own members and from Washington and the state capital. They have no police power. They have no direct control over land use, zoning, or building codes. Most of their decisions, therefore, have to be carried out by their constituent towns and counties—which may, or may not, be zealous in doing so. When a development district does get into direct operations—as in the case of Dayton's housing program—it is pretty much limited to service functions. When you come down to it, about the only authority a development district can exercise in its own right is the power of A-95 review: that is, the power in effect to cut off the flow of federal money. Strong as this can be, it is essentially a negative authority. For positive action, the district director and his staff have to depend on their skill in originating and packaging development projects—and their political craft in persuading local officials to go along with their plans.

As a result—in my observation at least—the development district idea works best in rural areas, where the problems to be solved are relatively uncomplicated and noncontroversial. Dayton's district, for instance, has few of the built-in conflicts that plague metropolitan areas—between white and black, between the core city and the suburbs, between rich and poor. The Georgia mountains have no big cities, few Negroes, and no serious class conflicts, since virtually everybody there (until recently, anyhow) was poor. Hence Dayton & Co. don't have to wrestle with such intractable assignments as the rehousing of slum families in suburbs that don't want them. The district can concentrate on straightforward development and conservation projects of obvious advantage to everybody. Or, to put it another way, its main job is the happy one of distributing federal money where it will do the most good. Much the same situation holds throughout the rural and semi-rural southern and Appalachian states.

Even there, however, the district councils tend to dodge the hard problems, simply because their structure is too fragile to handle them. I don't know of any district, for example, that has tried to forbid or regulate strip mining. Any that did almost certainly would be blown apart by the ensuing wrangle.

For the same reason, Councils of Government (as development districts are usually called in metropolitan areas) have been ineffectual in coping with the urgent—which means the controversial—crises of the cities. Sometimes they may even do more harm than good. Friends in San Francisco, whose judgment I respect in these matters, tell me that the existence of the Association of Bay Area Governments probably is a misfortune. It is too feeble to save the Bay region from the feverish speculative development that has ruined so much of San Mateo and Santa Clara counties and imperiled the Bay itself. Yet it has stood in the way of the development of a more adequate form of metropolitan government.

2. *Development districts are undemocratic.*

The delegates to their governing boards usually represent towns and counties, not individual citizens. The smallest village normally has a vote equal to that of the biggest city in the district. Thus a tiny minority can frustrate the will of the great majority. Such a setup plainly violates the one-man-one-vote principle laid down by the Supreme Court—and the first time it is challenged in the courts, it almost certainly will be ruled illegal. When that time comes, the whole system of development districts will face a painful choice: either to convert themselves into truly representative bodies or to become so purely "advisory" that their role will be almost meaningless.

A companion criticism is that the district governing boards are commonly dominated by the Establishment. Their membership is made up of elected officials, often with an additional spicing of local notables. The poor, the black, and the young, therefore, seldom are in evidence; and since a primary concern of the boards is economic development, they may be overly responsive to the wishes of the business community.

Plus

1. *The development districts have imposed some order on the chaotic welter of local governments.*

As the political scientists have been telling us for decades, a main reason for our loss of confidence in American society is the confusion and copelessness of local governments. We have too many of them—about eighty thousand, counting towns, counties, school districts, airport commissions, sanitary districts, and the almost endless list of other special-purpose agencies. A single piece of land may be taxed by as many as ten different layers of local government; and its owner, in theory, is expected to keep a watchful eye on all of them, and through his vote to keep them under some sort of democratic control. Clearly this is impossible, even if he were to spend full time on government-watching. The typical citizen, therefore, merely shrugs, curses "the politicians," and concludes that government is a hopeless mess.

He is right about the mess, at least, because virtually none of these eighty thousand units has the authority or jurisdiction to do a decent job. "Fragmented," "conflicting," and "overlapping" are perhaps the most frequently used words in the literature that has grown up about them. "Most American communities lack any instrumentality of government with legal powers, geographic jurisdiction, and independent revenue sources necessary to conduct local self-government in any valid sense." That is the judgment, not of some radical professor, but of the Committee for Economic Development, an organization of businessmen representing many of the country's biggest corporations. It recommended, among other things, that "at least 80 per cent" of the eighty thousand local governments should be abolished.*

That laudable goal obviously is politically impossible within the foreseeable future. For the average American voter is trapped in a psychological noose. He was brought up on the semi-anarchic doctrine that "That government is best which governs least"; he is disgusted with the performance of the governments he has; and he leaps to the conclusion that stronger and simpler government might be even worse. That fear of change is, of course, reinforced at every opportunity by the hundreds of thousands of petty local officials (most of them unnecessary) who fight like tigers to protect their own jobs and their patronage. As that Old Tiger, Clemenceau, liked to remind us: "There is no passion like that of the functionnaire for his function."

* Its 1966 report on "Modernizing Local Government" is still a classic, which should be required reading for every high school student and every grumbling taxpayer.

Given this cast of the public mind, the local development districts are at least a step forward. Since it is impossible, for the moment, to consolidate the clutter of local governments, the development district can at least coax and pressure them into working in harness. At its best, as in those districts we have examined, it can go a long way toward making local government effective.

2. *As a result, the districts can save a good deal of money for the taxpayers.*

Since Americans are incorrigibly addicted to forming associations—ranging from chess federations to the Society of Magazine Writers—it was inevitable that the district executives should set up an association of their own. Again we run up against that sticky problem of nomenclature. It is called the National Association of Regional Councils—and in its terminology, "regional council" means the same thing as "development district" or "Council of Governments" and all those other agencies of varying names but similar characteristics that I have been describing. (I have tried to avoid the term "region" because I wanted to save it to apply to a different kind of social innovation—federal regions, covering several states, which we shall encounter in a later chapter.)

Although the National Association of Regional Councils obviously is not disinterested in proclaiming the virtues of its member organizations, it is the best source of information we have about them. Its executive director, Richard C. Hartman, has estimated that in 1971 alone the districts saved $483 million in public funds, by stopping wasteful and overlapping projects during the course of A-95 review. This figure is accepted as being "within the ball park" by Dwight A. Ink, assistant director of the President's Office of Management and Budget—the man who probably knows more about such matters than anyone else in the country. (He is one of those unheralded but creative public servants who were responsible for inventing A-95 and nursing the development district idea into life.) I can find no reliable figures on what it cost to operate all the development districts that were working in 1971—but a reasonably informed guess is that the total was considerably less than the $483 million they saved.

3. *The districts are part of a curious movement now going on in many aspects of American life—a movement toward centralization and decentralization at the same time.*

In this double movement, I suspect, lies the salvation of American society, if it is to be saved.

We already have seen how this works in the case of the development districts. They are centralizing certain functions which local communities had been performing badly or not at all—planning, enticing new industry, protecting the environment. Simultaneously they are decentralizing certain decisions and responsibilities which the state capitals and Washington had been handling badly or not at all—the coordination of federal programs, in particular, and again the kind of practical planning necessary to build civilized communities.

In so doing, they have filled a vacuum. They are making decisions that nobody made before—and they have brought this decision-making reasonably close to the people whose lives are affected by it.

4. *They are helping to spread America's population more evenly over the landscape.*

By creating jobs and decent living conditions in hundreds of places that had neither, they make it possible for people to escape from the dehumanizing congestion of the great metropolises.

5. *They may be a necessary transitional step toward a simpler and more competent scheme of government.*

Even now some of the better development districts are getting their constituents accustomed to thinking bigger—

geographically, in terms of a community of a dozen counties, rather than a single county or village; in a time scale of years of development, rather than the date the next tax bill is due; socially, in terms of a unit big enough to tackle ambitious undertakings. Gradually they are eroding the popular mistrust of government—especially bigger and stronger government—because they patently are accomplishing something worthwhile and doing it without any noticeable resort to tyranny.

If this keeps on long enough, the public may recover from its endemic and destructive parochialism. It may be willing to let the development districts assume, little by little, the attributes of traditional government: the power to tax, the direct election of the governing councils, the exclusive jurisdiction over certain tasks that can only be handled on a district-wide basis, and the authority to make even controversial decisions stick. At the same time some of the redundant villages and sewage districts and local housing authorities may wither away or be absorbed into the larger structure. Then someday the dominant feature on the map of rural America may be the development district, rather than the county, simply because it has demonstrated that it works.

A similar kind of evolution already is under way in some metropolitan areas. The Puget Sound Governmental Conference is, despite its name, a Council of Governments: one of the earliest and most active. Although it suffers from all the structural weaknesses noted earlier, it has been able to do a good deal of effective planning for the cities and counties half-encircling the Sound. Late in 1972 it took a long step toward a structure both stronger and more democratic. It decided unanimously to base the voting strength of its members on population; Seattle, for instance, now has twenty-three votes, while smaller cities such as Bonney Lake and Snohomish have only one. Presumably this change will focus more attention on the problems of the central city. At the same time it should make the Conference's decisions more acceptable to the residents of Seattle, Tacoma, Everett, and Bremerton, who had been badly underrepresented in the past.

A recent proposal from the Southern California Association of Governments would go even further. It suggested that the state legislature should transform that COG into a general-purpose organization: something close to a genuine, though limited, governing body for the whole Los Angeles metropolitan area. Membership would become mandatory, rather than voluntary, for all the cities and counties within that area, and the organization would be endowed with its own sources of revenue. At this writing the California legislature has not acted on this proposal—but it does indicate one way a Council of Governments might evolve into a metropolitan government with real muscle.

There are other ways. The best of them so far, in my view, is being demonstrated in Minnesota.

5.

The Minnesota Experiment: How to Make a Big City Fit to Live In

Minnesota is the best-governed state in America. It also is the most imaginative, farsighted, and ambitious. Its finest contribution to the art of politics—the latest of many—is a new kind of metropolitan government, more sophisticated and successful than anything of the kind attempted elsewhere. Already it is being recognized as a beacon for the rest of the country—and even for people overseas, from Tokyo to London, who are searching for some way to make their giant cities livable.

When I first heard this kind of talk, from an assortment of Minnesota politicians, businessmen, and professors, I listened with tolerant amusement. It sounded like old-timey frontier bragging, tinctured with the naïve Chamber of Commerce boosterism that went out of style along with George Babbitt. Odd, isn't it, that his sales pitch should continue to echo for so long on his native prairie?

But after several years of watching what is actually happening in Minnesota, I have come to suspect that its local patriots may be speaking something close to the literal truth. Maybe it really *is* the best-governed state. And I am persuaded that it has invented something which may prove as significant to American cities as the Wright brothers' first plane was to aviation.

This device is known as the Twin Cities Metropolitan Council. It is providing unified direction for a whole urban

region: a domain including 1,800,000 people—nearly half
the state's population—its two big cities, Minneapolis and
St. Paul; about 130 smaller municipalities in the surrounding countryside; seven counties; a worm-can of special-
purpose agencies; and (eventually) a zoo. In design and
concept it is quite different from other experiments in
metropolitan government, such as those in Nashville, Tennessee; Miami and Jacksonville in Florida; and Toronto in
Canada. Already it is so successful that comparable designs
are being evolved (with appropriate local variations) in
Atlanta and Seattle. And I think it likely that it will be
imitated by at least a dozen other metropolitan regions
before the end of the century.

Why is this happening in Minnesota, instead of in New
York, Illinois, or California, where the urban crisis is so
much more acute? One explanation, cited by nearly everyone I talked to in Minnesota, is the state's unique political
tradition.

To begin with, it has an unusually homogeneous population, mostly of Scandinavian, German, and Yankee descent.
Its racial problems are relatively minor; less than 2 per cent
of its residents are black, Latins are a rarity, and the most
troubled minority is the remnant of the native Indian tribes.
The original settlers were nearly all farmers, who took a
lively and responsible interest in the affairs of their own
small communities. No one industry ever dominated the
state—as mining, for instance, dominated West Virginia.
There the coal companies traditionally have run things
(often in the interest of absentee owners) and also have
paid the biggest share of the tax bill. Many of West Virginia's little people, the mine workers and the creek-bed
farmers, have accepted this semi-feudal society; so long as
they don't have to pay for government they are content to let
somebody else manage it, however badly.

To the typical Minnesotans, such passivity would be unthinkable. For reasons I don't fully understand, they always have been intensely ambitious, not only for themselves but for their society. Maybe the fact that Easterners and even Chicagoans long regarded them as a bunch of yokels may have had something to do with it. Anyhow, they have been almost obsessively anxious to prove that they belong in the big leagues; and to get there they have been willing to pay whatever it takes, in both energy and cash. As a consequence, although they have only 2 per cent of the country's population, they have built the fourth-largest university system, several excellent liberal arts colleges, a symphony orchestra respected throughout the world, the Tyrone Guthrie Theater, and three art galleries of some distinction. They have produced medical pioneers at both the Mayo Clinic and the university medical school, famed for its leadership in heart surgery. In business their innovations range from Scotch tape to bank holding companies, with the result that poverty is not a really aggravating problem. They have supported superior newspapers and architects. They have even insisted on acquiring big-league teams in baseball and football—an insistence which, in a curious fashion, helped lead to the Metropolitan Council.

As elsewhere, prestige goes along with money; but in Minnesota even more prestige comes from conspicuous public service. The business leaders, and a good many intellectuals and professional men, therefore devote a remarkable amount of their time to good works. The archetypical man-who-has-made-it in, say, Miami may enjoy his leisure on a yacht, or in Hollywood among his collection of starlets—but if he lived in Minneapolis he would spend it in committee meetings.*

---

* Donald Dayton, one of the owners of Minneapolis' leading department stores, recently retired in vigorous middle age to devote his full time to public service. I happened to attend a conference on metropolitan government where he was one of the panelists; he more

Moreover, this is young people's country. The whole power structure—in government, politics, and business—is run predominantly by men in their thirties and forties. Unlike those in California and Florida, it is not weighed down with a mass of timid, tired, and conservative old people—perhaps because so many of them move to a warmer climate as soon as they retire. A visitor quickly gets a sense that all institutions are open to change, and know it has to come. Both dinner table conversations and public debate are likely to focus on the nature and direction of the coming changes, not the question of whether they are desirable.

The political parties, in particular, are free of the encrusted machinery and tribal gerontocracy that are so frustrating to young activists in many states. "Clean government" has long been taken for granted. Since politics offers virtually no patronage or opportunity for graft, the two parties—which are pretty well even in strength—have to concentrate on issues rather than spoils. In this competition, both have become relatively liberal. And since a permanent machine can't survive without patronage, newcomers to politics do not have to buck a hierarchy of entrenched bosses. They can get into the action immediately and rise fast. It is no accident that Minnesota produced Senators Hubert Humphrey, Gene McCarthy, and Walter Mondale in a single political generation—or that a pack of able youngsters is crowding up behind them.

---

than held his own, intellectually, with the civil servants and government professors who served on the panel with him. On our way to dinner that evening, one of my friends remarked casually that "Dayton's is the best department store in America. It makes Neiman-Marcus look *parvenu*." Since I am no judge of department stores, I pass this observation along simply as an example of local self-confidence.

A few years ago I would have guessed that Minneapolis and St. Paul could never get together on anything, least of all a joint system of government. With their downtown centers only fifteen miles apart, on opposite banks of the Mississippi River, they had always been implacable rivals. This mutual jealousy began to subside only when both of them were hit over the head, so to speak, with a baseball bat. Each, in an effort to get ahead of the other, tried to get a major-league baseball franchise. Both were rebuffed. To their chagrin they realized that they could not get or support a big-league team in baseball—or football, or hockey— unless they operated it jointly as a Twin Cities venture. Thus on the sports pages appeared the first sprouts of civic wisdom.

Meanwhile, more serious problems were getting out of hand. The most noisome one was sewage. More than 300,000 people on the outskirts of the two cities were pumping their water out of backyard wells, and pouring their sewage into backyard cesspools. They were horrified to discover, in 1959, that half of their wells were contaminated—and that pollution was threatening the region's lakes and rivers, as well as its shallow underground water table. Because it is physically impossible to build efficient sewage disposal systems on a piecemeal, suburb-by-suburb basis, community leaders began to talk about a sanitary district covering the entire urban region.

At the same time the two cities and their surrounding small towns were getting increasingly worried about other troubles, which no one of them could handle alone. Polluted air was blowing from the factory districts into the residential suburbs. Outlying land had to be earmarked for future parks and open space before it was overrun by urban sprawl. The routing of throughways and location of a new airport would affect everyone in the region. A rapid-transit system to link together the Twin Cities and their satellite communities would soon become indispensable. The population of the area seemed likely to double before the end of the century: where should the homes and schools and shopping centers for these newcomers be located?* Each of these questions hooked up with every other. How, for example, could anyone decide where to put water and sewer lines, until it was clear where the future population and industrial centers would be? The growth of these centers in turn would depend largely on the location of highway and transit routes. Yet nobody—no official, no institution—was authorized to decide these questions in such a way that the answers would mesh together into a sensible overall pattern.

The political theorists have a standard prescription for situations such as this: all of the hundreds of governmental units within the region ought to merge together into a single all-purpose metropolitan government. The only trouble with this remedy is that it is impossible to apply. Wherever it has been proposed—St. Louis, Seattle, and San Francisco are typical examples—it has been defeated. Local officials fight it because they are afraid of losing their jobs. Suburbanites fear they will have to pay higher taxes to meet the soaring school and welfare costs of the central city. They also are afraid of losing control of their own schools and zoning regulations to faceless bureaucrats downtown. One result of metropolitan government, they suspect, would be the building of subsidized housing for the poor in the middle-class neighborhoods—thus raising school and welfare costs, and quite possibly the crime rate as well. County legislators don't

* Although Minnesota was still growing briskly in the early seventies, a possible limit to its future growth had suddenly come in sight. Some industrial planners were suggesting that because of the nation's energy crisis, few large-scale industries were likely to locate that far north in coming decades, simply because they will be too expensive to heat. One of them told me in 1973 that he was no longer recommending any factory sites north of Kansas City.

want the wicked city to become more powerful; therefore, better keep it divided and impotent. Downtown politicians, on the other hand, are not eager to share their power with their suburban counterparts—particularly since the city machine is likely to be Democratic, while most suburbanites are Republican. Many citizens are simply frightened of Big Government in any form. And a few kooks will always arise to denounce any Metro proposal as a Communist plot.

Knowing that such opposition would be insuperable, the Minnesota power structure didn't even bother to suggest consolidation of local units into an all-purpose metropolitan government. They proposed something quite different: a Metropolitan Council with its authority strictly limited to those few functions that clearly *had* to be handled on an area-wide basis. It would not mess around with the zoning code in Wayzata or with the way Bloomington runs its school system. Each little town would continue to manage its police and street lighting and traffic rules exactly as it pleased. No village councilman need worry about losing his job or his dignity. No politician need feel that his power base was in jeopardy.

But in those few fields where it would be given responsibility—sewage and water supply, airport location, highway routes, preservation of open space, mass transit, and the like—the Council would have real authority. Unlike the Councils of Governments in most metropolitan areas, it would not have to reach decisions by unanimous consent. It would have its own sources of revenue, so it would not have to depend on voluntary contributions from 150-odd municipalities and counties. It would have responsibility for making overall plans "for the orderly physical, social, and economic growth of the Twin Cities area." Moreover, it would review all plans and projects of local governments and special agencies, such as the Airports Commission. If it found that any of them conflicted with the regional plan, the Council could suspend them. It also would be empowered to review local requests for federal aid, under the A-95 clearinghouse authority mentioned in the previous chapter.

Obviously such a Council would not be a scary, all-powerful superoctopus—which is what the conventional scheme for metropolitan government usually sounds like. It would have just enough clout to make essential decisions, on matters of vital regional concern, that nobody had been authorized to make in the past.

The proposed Council was to be unique in yet another way: its seventeen members would not represent any existing units of government. Sixteen of them would be selected from specially created districts of roughly equal population, while the chairman would be selected at large. Consequently no member would have to feel that his first duty was to look out for the parochial interests of, say, Eden Prairie or Ramsey County. Thus freed from local patriotisms and pressures, they could afford to think about the interests of the region as a whole.

This concept had no single father. It grew out of seemingly interminable discussions among businessmen, officeholders, and civic groups over a period of eighteen years— and these powwows probably would never have come to much if the sewage and water problems had not become intolerable. (Fischer's Law: In American politics nothing much happens until the status quo becomes more painful than change. We shall see how this applies in Jacksonville and other communities, just as surely as in Minnesota.)

A big piece of the credit for the Council scheme, however, belongs to the Citizens League, an independent, nonpartisan organization working for better government. Most Good Government organizations are, of course, notoriously ineffectual—merely goo-goos, in the contemptuous phrase of the famous Senator Plunkett of Tammany Hall. The Citizens League is an exception.

Its executive secretary is Ted Kolderie, a lean, intense young man who had spent ten years as a reporter and editorial writer for the Minneapolis *Star,* specializing in local government. Unlike the garden variety of do-gooder, he is not only idealistic but politically sophisticated; and he is endowed with boundless energy, plus bottomless patience. When he loses a fight, he does not give up in despair and take to reading the thoughts of Chairman Mao; he splashes cold water on his face, takes a deep breath, and gets ready for the next round.

Behind him he has an equally uncommon organization. The president at the time the Council idea was hatched was Francis M. Boddy, a professor of economics at the University of Minnesota. Its directors are a choice selection of the region's public-spirited businessmen, energetic women, and academic intellectuals. There isn't a political innocent among them, and nearly all of the directors—and the 3,600 members—are willing to devote a lot of time to unglamorous, toilsome assignments. They, and the League's small staff, were in good part responsible for working out the details of the Metropolitan Council plan and winning the support of innumerable local officeholders, Chambers of Commerce, and neighborhood associations.

In 1967 the reform strategists made a key decision: to ask the legislature to enact their proposal into law. If they had chosen instead to carry it directly to the voters by way of referendum—a more common procedure—it might well have been defeated. Explaining such a complex scheme to hundreds of thousands of busy citizens—most of them either indifferent or nervous about the idea—is always difficult; and because it is necessarily complicated and unfamiliar, it is highly vulnerable to misleading attacks by its opponents.

The reformers also felt strongly that their plan was properly business for the legislature, rather than the populace at large. Only there could it be scrutinized line by line by men skilled in the craft of government, and if necessary refined and clarified. Furthermore, local governments of whatever scale are creatures of the state, and the legislators have a constitutional responsibility to see to it that they work. The fact that legislatures have often been callous or hostile to the metropolises does not lessen this responsibility; it is all the more reason for concerned citizens to make them face up to their job. So at least was the reasoning of the Citizens League.

Oddly enough, the enabling act was introduced by Senator Gordon Rosenmeier of Little Falls, a leader of the rural clique that had dominated the Minnesota legislature for as long as anybody could remember. Although he is a mistruster of cities, he could see that power was shifting fast from the country to the urban precincts. Evidently he figured that it would be better to settle now for a relatively tame and limited form of Metro government, rather than risk the creation of an uncontrollable monster a few years later. Besides, like most of his colleagues, he did not like the only visible alternative: that is, for the legislature itself to try to cope with the tangled and politically thorny problems of the metropolis.

After prolonged debate, the legislature voted in 1967, with the support of both parties, to set up the Metropolitan Council in much the form the reformers had envisaged. True enough, the Citizen Leaguers did not get everything they wanted. For instance, they had urged that members of the Council should be elected. This was defeated by a tie vote in the Senate, with the result that the original members of the Council were appointed by the governor. The issue did not die, however. It has been debated in every subsequent session of the legislature, and it now seems likely that Council membership eventually will be changed from an appointive to an elective office.

The legislature did, however, give the newborn government the essential tools it needed to start work:

1. Money—about $725,000 a year to begin with, to be raised by a half-mill tax levied on property throughout the metropolitan area. In addition, close to $500,000 a year has been scrounged from Washington in planning grants.

2. A staff—mostly taken over from an already existing planning commission that had done some good research, but had no power to put its ideas into operation. Its executive director is Robert T. Jorvig, an able civil servant who had studied planning at the University of Minnesota and Harvard. The fact that he had worked both for St. Paul and Minneapolis in responsible positions made him acceptable to both cities.

3. Teeth—in the form of authority to review, and in some cases to suspend, the projects put forward by other governments and special-purpose agencies. (It has used this authority more vigorously than most legislators had expected—to the considerable pain of Mr. Rosenmeier, for one. He told me recently that he never had anticipated that the Council would develop the muscular authority it is exercising today.)

4. A well-defined mission—to take a hard look at the most pressing problems of the region, and to decide what ought to be done about them, in what order, by whom, and how to pay the bill. It also was instructed to report back to the legislature if further action there should be needed to carry out the plan.

To serve as chairman of the new Twin Cities Metropolitan Council, then-Governor Harold Le Vander chose James L. Hetland, a forty-three-year-old law professor at the University of Minnesota. He had never held public office, although he had been an active worker in the liberal wing of the Republican Party. It proved to be a fortunate appointment, for Hetland not only nursed the Council through the perilous years of its infancy with shrewdness and tact, he also set the fundamental policies which have guided it ever since.

When I first met Hetland he was trying to handle most of his Council business out of an overheated little office in the law school, his heels propped up on a desk littered with examination papers and planning documents. He is built like a welterweight, with the face of an Irish ward leader and a deceptively relaxed manner. Nobody, obviously, could really be that relaxed when he carried a full teaching load in one of the better law schools and also worked at least forty hours a week for the Council. For this "part-time" work he got paid a modest salary; the other members of the Council got only per diem expenses. In the peculiar social climate of Minnesota it is easier to recruit good men for the tough jobs as volunteers, and their word commands more respect than it would if they were paid officeholders.

As Hetland explained to me, the Council never expected to build and operate sewage lines, transit systems, and the like itself. Instead it was to serve as a kind of holding company, laying down broad policy guidelines and supervising a group of subordinate agencies that would carry out the detailed planning, construction, and day-to-day operation of the regional facilities. Some of these already existed—for example, the quasi-independent Airports and Transit Commissions. Others would have to be created to handle such things as air pollution, garbage disposal, and—of all things —a zoo. (I found it rather touching that so many Minnesotans feel that a really first-class metropolis ought to have a first-class zoo, just as it ought to have a theater, a symphony, and big-league sports teams. Since the zoo would be used by everybody in the region, they think it only logical that it should be financed and managed as a regional project.)

That is, in fact, about the way things have worked out, although the going has not always been smooth. Sewage was no great problem from an administrative point of view. Under the Council's direction, a Metropolitan Waste Control Board took over the ownership of all major treatment plants and collection lines within the region, abolished a clutter of little independent sewer districts, and issued $71 million worth of bonds to build new lines and treatment plants. As a result, the lakes, rivers, and underground water table are already almost completely cleaned up—a major ecological victory.

But as might be expected, some of the old and powerful independent agencies had no mind to accept the Council's authority without a struggle. The first big fight was over the location of a new airport. Twice the Airports Commission came up with site proposals that struck the Council as unsatisfactory, because of potential damage to the environment and lack of control over development of the surrounding areas. Twice the Council made its vetoes stick—although not until it had gone back to the legislature for additional authority to regulate land use around the perimeter of the future airport. At this writing, the Council and Commission seem close to agreement on a third site that will meet all the Council's environmental requirements and also will fit into the Council's plans for the overall future development of the region. Perhaps most important, the Council came out of this scrap with its authority clarified and its prestige increased.

A similar hassle developed with the Transit Commission, and has been resolved in the same way: with the legislature upholding the Council's powers to set policy guidelines and to order the Commission to carry them out. Indeed, the legislature has gone even further. It has given the Council authority to appoint the members of most of the operating commissions, and to review their annual budgets—thus giving the Council direct, positive control over the operating agencies, as well as its original power of veto. On three occasions, in 1969, 1971, and 1974, the legislature acted to enlarge and strengthen the functions of the Council, and, if necessary, it probably will do so again. As one of the state's wisest political observers recently told me:

"The status of the Council is still in the process of evolution. But it does seem to have established itself firmly in the confidence of the legislature and of most of the voters in the state. It may have to go through a few more fights to resolve some of the conflicts still outstanding—but it's a good bet the Council eventually will end up with whatever muscle it needs to do its job."

So far it has done its job remarkably well. Hetland left the chairmanship in 1971 to become vice-president in charge of urban development for the First National Bank of Minneapolis, an institution with a strong commitment to improving the quality of life of the region. He is now, in effect, directing the use of private capital to help carry through the plans he initiated through the Council in its early years. Subsequent chairmen have kept on Jorvig and his able professional staff, and the innovative thrust of the organization seems undiminished.

In the few years since its founding in 1967, the Council has chalked up a considerable list of accomplishments. It has solved the sewage and water problems for the seven-county metropolis. It has reorganized garbage disposal, closing down forty-two old dumps and opening up fifteen new landfill areas. It has stopped the wild proliferation of super-highways, and is well on the way to launching a modern mass-transit system. (In the beginning probably buses, moving in streets or lanes reserved for them alone; later, perhaps, some sort of new-technology "people movers.") It has stopped the draining of wetlands, the pollution of lakes—

one of Minnesota's most attractive assets—and the building of homes on flood plains. (It refused to permit the building of sewer lines to serve tracts subject to flooding: a simple, costless decision. If similar decisions had been taken elsewhere in the Mississippi Valley before the 1973 inundations, they would have prevented hundreds of millions of dollars in damages.)

One of the Council's most courageous actions was to force the wealthy suburbs to build low- and medium-income housing in limited but significant amounts. Here again it used its A-95 review power; if a community failed to include low-income housing in its development plan, the whole plan got turned down. (To be sure, the Council didn't phrase it this bluntly, and so far no plan has actually been vetoed. A delicate hint in the early consultation stage has been enough.)

An innovation that may have incalculable influence, eventually, on the rest of the country is a scheme to equalize property taxes throughout the region. It has damped down the competition between communities to increase their tax base by attracting new factories and office buildings—and thus has made it easier for the Council to plan the rational location of industrial developments. How this ingenious idea works can best be discussed later on, together with other types of tax reform.

The heart of the Council's operations is its Development Guide—an overall plan to ensure "a visually pleasing, coherent, and workable environment" for the entire region. This Guide is not yet completed—indeed, in one sense it never will be because it is subject to continuous refinement and revision—but its main components already are in place. They are embodied in a series of documents, formally adopted and published by the Council after months of staff work, public hearings, and consultation with private-interest groups and other public agencies. Each one deals with a major topic: housing, transportation, finance, and so on.

Unlike many planning documents they are (for the most part) written in layman's English and printed in a handsome format; together they make a useful starting library for anyone interested in planning.

If the Guide did not exist, the Twin Cities area probably would look by the end of the century much like New Jersey does today. It would double its population by sprawling mindlessly over the countryside, in a muddle of ticky-tack real estate developments, filling stations, trailer parks, factories, merchandising malls, quick-food eateries, motels, billboards, and secondhand car lots—the whole mess crisscrossed by highways and shrouded in perpetual smog. This is the typically American form of chaos; you can find a sample on the outskirts of practically any big city.

But there is no law of God or man that says a metropolis has to grow like a cancer. It is possible for it to grow rationally and humanely; and the Development Guide is an effort to make sure that at least one metropolis will do so.

To this end, it proposes to concentrate most of the future growth in sixteen "centers." Six of them already exist: the central business districts of Minneapolis and St. Paul, and four towns lying beyond them in a roughly circular pattern. Ten new "centers" are to be developed during the next quarter of a century. Each of them will be a small city, providing anywhere from a few hundred to thirty thousand jobs.

Each of them will also provide, within a compact area, everything needed for a civilized life: shopping centers, community colleges, recreation, industrial parks, some high-density housing. All sixteen centers will be linked to each other by the present highway network and the coming rapid-transit system; additional road building will be held to a minimum. Future auto traffic may, in fact, be reduced because most families will find most everything close at hand. It will no longer be necessary for a housewife to drive ten miles east for her groceries, five miles south to get the kids to school, and eight miles north to the hairdresser, while her husband travels twenty miles twice a day to and from work.

Most of the land between the centers will remain open space: farms, parks, playing fields, lakes, and forest.

With one exception, the centers will not be new towns. (The exception is Jonathan, a new town now a-building.) They are simply planned developments of localities which already have shown potential for natural growth. Their future is to be shaped by all the tools that the Council and other units of government can use to influence the direction of development.

An arsenal of such tools is at hand—location of sewage lines, tax incentives, zoning, the siting of transit terminals, and the like. But experience over the next few years is likely to indicate, I believe, that additional instruments will be needed. In particular, public agencies may have to acquire tighter control over the use of land—as Vermont, Delaware, and a few other states are beginning to do. Some farmland, for example, will have to be kept for farming, even if the owner could make more money by selling it off for a shopping center or seventy-five-foot residential lots. Under the present weak zoning laws, such preservation of land for its best use in the public interest is difficult, and often impossible.

The Council will, of course, be under constant pressure to let its Development Guide be eroded. Powerful financial and political interests will inevitably push for amendments and exceptions—to put a transit terminal in a slightly wrong place because the site change will give somebody a million-dollar windfall, or to sacrifice just one more small piece of open space for a real estate development. If the Council (or the counties and municipalities which are largely responsible for carrying out its plans) yield too often to such pressures, the grand design for the Twin Cities metropolis can become a mess: just one more planners' dream gone wrong.

I am reasonably hopeful that this will not happen, however, simply because too many Minnesotans own a piece of the dream. As noted earlier, they have large ambitions for their rather special society. They know that in the Metropolitan Council they are building an institution both original and of exceptional promise; and quite a lot of them are determined to make it work.

In 1972 the Urban Institute, a private research organization in Washington, D.C., issued a report titled: "A Study in Comparative Urban Indicators: Conditions in 18 Large Metropolitan Areas." It undertook a rough measure of the quality of life in each of these eighteen areas, according to twelve yardsticks—how many families below the poverty line, how much unemployment, the crime rate, the level of educational achievement, air quality, infant mortality, the suicide rate, citizen participation in public affairs, cost of housing, per capita income, transportation costs, and community concern as indicated by response to United Fund appeals. A composite ranking of these indicators showed that the Twin Cities metropolitan area led all the rest in quality of life.

Naturally citizens of the area are proud of this ranking. They hope to stay No. 1 through the rest of this century and beyond; and if they do, some of the credit will belong to their invention of their Metropolitan Council—not just as an instrument of government, but as a potent means of enhancing the quality of life.

6.

The Possibly Glorious Dream of Gloria M. Segal

At the risk of sounding like a press agent, I have to point out that the state of Minnesota is remarkable for private innovations as well as the public one discussed in the last chapter.

Like thousands of other energetic matrons whose children have grown out from underfoot, Mrs. Gloria M. Segal began to dabble in real estate. Typically, such dabblers end up as partners in an agency, selling a couple of split-levels a month. Not Mrs. S. To her own bemusement, she now finds herself serving as den mother for a new community that eventually may house 30,000 people. The first 1,300 residents moved in early in 1973, but to complete the town, Mrs. Segal and her associates expect to spend up to $30 million a year over the next two decades, some of it their own money.

If this large, economy-size dabble works out according to Mrs. Segal's dream, it could change the life-style of millions of Americans. For Mrs. Segal hopes to create not only better homes, but a new kind of urban environment—a potential model for much of the building this country must undertake during the next half century. (It will not be the sort of environment I would choose, but Jane Jacobs and the Rolling Stones should love it.) Even if it falls short—and the risks are high—its failures should tell us something well worth learning.

If some things do go wrong, it will not be for want of vision. Mrs. Segal has enough vision to outfit Joan of Arc, Joan Baez, and all of the Brook Farm utopians.

Her dream is taking shape on a hundred acres of run-down real estate at the eastern edge of Minneapolis. It is called Cedar-Riverside, after the two main streets that intersect there. It is the first new-town-in-town to be undertaken under the federal New Communities program. In looks, physical workings, and social patterns, it will be quite different from any project you have ever seen. Item: rich and poor families will live together in the same building and in similar apartments, with nothing to show which family pays the maximum $500 a month rent and which pays the minimum $50. Item: the project already has a thicker concentration of experimental theaters, handicraft shops, dance groups, leather boutiques, coffeehouses, and alternative culture hangouts than any community I know of between Greenwich Village and San Francisco. Mrs. Segal enjoys that kind of scene and has invested considerable money and ingenuity in fostering it. A little raffishness, she feels, helps make a city exciting.

The plan calls for a high-density community, packing in more living units (about 120) per acre than some congested sections of Manhattan. Yet it will (so the vision goes) offer light, air, architectural distinction, playgrounds, and safety from muggers, automobiles, and suburban boredom, plus all the cultural amenities of a great city, from swimming pools to art galleries. The residents will be a rich mix of ethnic groups, middle-class professionals and poor people, artists and housewives, students and businessmen, the young and the elderly. Most of them are expected to walk to work at the universities, hospitals, and offices close at hand, or in downtown Minneapolis, only twelve blocks away. Others will travel via the Twin Cities rapid-transit system, now in the planning stage; or perhaps by "people movers" or "horizontal elevators"—still only a gleam in Mrs. Segal's wide brown eyes. Unavoidable auto traffic will be completely separated from pedestrians, who will move through a complex of plazas, parks, and covered walkways linking all buildings at second- and third-story levels.

For women residents especially, living habits will change. Unlike the suburban housewife who spends much of her day chauffeuring children to school, doctors, and playmates, the young mother in Cedar-Riverside will have day-care centers, schools, and playgrounds within strolling distance in her own "neighborhood." (The community will be divided into five such "neighborhoods," each with its own grocery, drugstore, laundry, and similar services. The first is now close to completion.) A twenty-four-hour health service will also be available in neighborhood clinics, sponsored by the nearby hospitals. For major shopping and recreation, one can go to The Centrum, a combination of Main Street and the classic Greek agora, at about the middle of the project. It will incorporate some of the better old buildings still standing—for example, a nineteenth-century firehouse now converted into a neighborhood social center, and Dania Hall, an abandoned clubhouse of the same vintage, with a ballroom and theater.

Two-way television, for which conduits are being laid as the buildings go up, could also change life-styles.

"If you are not feeling well," Mrs. Segal explained, "you can flick on your TV and report to the local health station. And you might do your shopping the same way. You could make up your grocery order from a list on the TV screen, a computer would register it, and in due course a box would appear at your door."

The same circuits might also be used for a community forum, among families relaxing in their own living rooms, or for reporting prowlers, or for police surveillance of problem areas.

Other technological innovations are less far out. One of them is a new kind of heating plant, developed in co-operation with two local utility companies, that can serve up to four thousand dwelling units, at low cost and with little or no environmental pollution.

To some observers, including myself, a lot of this sounds, well, visionary. The plans and models reminded me a little of Piranesi's dream structures or of the anthill-like "acrologies" fantasized by Paolo Soleri. I am not at all sure that life in such a compacted environment will turn out to be as cozy and joyous as the Cedar-Riverside brochures suggest. There is some evidence, admittedly inconclusive, that personal stress and anti-social behavior tend to increase in step with population density and that crime rates in apartment buildings go up in rough accordance with their heights.* (Some of the Cedar-Riverside structures will run to thirty and forty stories.) Moreover, the first apartments put on display to potential renters struck me as smallish, at least for families with a couple of children, though they might be fine for young singles. Their balconies are a nice decorative

* Both crime rates and the behavior of residents also are strongly influenced by the way a building is designed and sited. How this works is brilliantly demonstrated in a recent book, *Defensible Space* (Macmillan, $8.95), by Oscar Newman, director of the Institute of Planning and Housing at New York University. Certain types of buildings—notably those put up in many public-housing projects— are open invitations to muggers, burglars, and vandals. Other types, no more expensive and at least as pleasing aesthetically, are far safer and more pleasant to live in. This holds true not only for low-income housing but also for "luxury" apartments. In view of Newman's findings it is hard to imagine anyone ever again building one of those monumental-slabs-in-a-barren-landscape beloved by Le Corbusier and other celebrated architects of his school.
I am not sure how thoroughly the Cedar-Riverside planners have absorbed Newman's lessons, but I'm confident that they will take them into account in the designs of at least the later stages of their new town.

touch, but they are too narrow to hold even a single chair. And from my own scant experience with computers, I would confidently expect a televised grocery order for a head of lettuce to produce a dozen pigs' feet and a case of champagne. Plenty of other questions, financial as well as architectural and social, cannot be finally answered for years.

Yet Mrs. Segal and her associates might just bring it off. Already they have accomplished things that any sensible land developer would consider impossible: in the assembly of their land, for example, the relocation of its occupants, and the manipulation of some thirty-five city, state, and federal agencies, not to mention bankers and investors. On the record so far, I would not bet against Gloria on anything she really wants to get done.

The record begins in 1962 when, as Mrs. Segal says, "I was looking for a tax-sheltered investment." (She likes to come on as a hard-nosed businesswoman because, I suspect, she is afraid her bubbling idealism might put off men of practical affairs. In fact, that idealism is her greatest asset, and she really isn't capable of concealing it.) Her husband Martin, a prosperous but by no means wealthy doctor, went along cheerfully, as he had with her earlier enthusiasms for music and for Democratic politics. He has never taken an active part, however, in her real estate ventures.

On the advice of a friend, Keith Heller, who taught accounting and tax law at the University of Minnesota business school, she used $19,000 of the family savings to buy an equity in an aging apartment house. Once refurbished and refinanced, it yielded a comfortable return.

At about this time Mrs. Segal was annoyed because she had a hard time finding parking places near the university concert hall. Heller suggested that she buy a vacant lot in Cedar-Riverside—then a semi-slum where land was dirt cheap, but still within easy walking distance of the university by footbridge over the Mississippi. She did, and vastly enjoyed her private parking lot.

She also wondered why it had come so cheap. Cedar-Riverside had once been a respectable though poor community, settled a hundred years ago by Scandinavian and Eastern European immigrants. (Mrs. Segal's uncle ran a grocery there.) But gradually it turned into a honky-tonk district, infested with lumberjacks on a spree, alcoholics, whores, and assorted bums. Cedar Avenue became known as Snoose Boulevard, after the Swedish word for the tobacco juice that splattered its sidewalks. As the stable families moved out, the population fell from twenty thousand to four thousand; many of the old one- and two-story frame houses stood empty; shops, except for the shabby bars, were mostly boarded up.

On the other hand the district lies just between the business centers of Minneapolis and St. Paul, both expanding rapidly. It is bordered by two new interstate highways. On its outskirts are two small colleges, two hospitals, and the giant University of Minnesota—which in 1959 began to reach across the river to establish a new West Campus in Cedar-Riverside. A little later the city designated it as an urban renewal area and announced plans for a good-sized park along the riverbank.

Mrs. Segal and Professor Heller smelled a bargain. They decided to buy up a few more of those cheap lots and build a small apartment building for rental to students, faculty members, and employees of the neighboring hospitals.

When they consulted Ralph Rapson, now head of the university's architectural school, he didn't think much of the idea. "Peanuts," he said. Why not buy up still more of the land while the going was good, and then tackle something really big—like a housing complex of architectural distinction and real social value?

So Mrs. Segal remortgaged her original apartment house and used the money to buy additional properties. By this time she and Heller were partners in Cedar-Riverside Associates, Inc., and gradually they brought in other investors, now totaling about fifty-five. The firm rehabilitated some of the old homes it bought, rented and remortgaged them, and put the proceeds into still more acreage, until it owned or controlled about 85 per cent of the privately held property in Cedar-Riverside: in all, some five hundred separate parcels.

Meanwhile, the original vision was growing like the fairy-tale beanstalk. Instead of building one dinky apartment or even a housing complex, the Associates were now bent on creating a whole new town. It seemed prudent, then, to bring in somebody who knew something about new towns— and about coping with the multitudinous arms of government that inevitably would become involved. They turned to Henry T. McKnight, a former state senator, a Republican (to offset the known liberalism of the Segal-Heller combo), a noted conservationist, the father of the state park system, a friend of Hubert Humphrey's, a successful land developer—and, most significantly, the founder of Jonathan, a new town a-building about twenty-five miles southwest of Minneapolis. McKnight became chairman of Cedar-Riverside Associates, with Heller (who had left his university job) as president and Mrs. Segal as vice-president and cheerleader.

From then on the enterprise proceeded as a curious partnership between the Associates and government. They never tried to fight City Hall: instead they seduced it—so successfully that the city council passed twelve new ordinances in a single day, June 4, 1971, to loosen the straitjacket of zoning and building codes. To direct the planning, the Associates brought in Donald A. Jacobson, who had many years of similar experience with the Minneapolis Housing and Redevelopment Authority. A former mayor, Arthur Naftalin,

became a consultant. Their know-how in dealing with government—and McKnight's—made possible the intricate
arrangements for financing the project. The key to it is a
$24-million guarantee to private investors under the federal
New Communities program, but the project also taps half a
dozen other sources of public funds, local and national,
including rent subsidies for low-income families. In similar
fashion, every step in the physical planning is being worked
out hand in hand with public agencies, from the state highway department to the university.

Urban renewal has become a hateful term in many cities
because it has so often meant the destruction of existing
neighborhoods and the uprooting of thousands of poor families. Mrs. Segal and her partners were determined that
nothing of the sort would happen in Cedar-Riverside. Of the
150 people they have had to move so far, all but two have
been resettled within the community—in better quarters
and with no increase in rents. This was possible because the
Associates had bought up nearly all the old homes in the
area, many of them vacant, and had rehabilitated them for
this express purpose. By the time the last of them is torn
down, twenty-five years from now, all the residents will have
had a chance to move into the new buildings.

Meanwhile they are being handled with extraordinary
tact. A case in point is that of the sixteen old men. They had
lived together for years in an old frame house. When its site
had to be cleared, they were offered apartments in a housing
project for elderly people that already had gone up a few
blocks away. "Hell, no," they said in effect. "We don't want
to move into that coop full of chattering old women. We
want to stay right where we are. We are used to each other,
and we are used to our own home, such as it is."

So Mrs. Segal came up with an alternative plan that they
accepted with gratitude. One night they all went to a hotel

for dinner, a party, and an overnight stay, at the Associates' expense. Next morning they went back to their old house, where they found everything in its accustomed place, down to the last beer bottle. But the house had been moved during the night to new foundations on a vacant lot a few hundred feet down the street; for them the only change was the view.

Such delicacy perhaps accounts for the fact that the Associates, landlords for four thousand people, have never had a rent strike or used a rent collector. "All rents come in over the counter or in the mail," Mrs. Segal said, "and we have less than 1 per cent uncollected. That's fantastic."

Another reason for their comfortable relationship with their tenants is that the Associates, particularly Mrs. Segal, have made themselves part of the community. Their unpretentious office is in the middle of it, in what used to be an ice cream factory. Mrs. Segal is accessible to anybody with a question, a gripe, or an idea for the project; and many of her evenings are spent discussing plans and problems with neighborhood groups. If a student commune wants to repaint its house with purple flowers and green peace symbols —as several of them have—she comes up with paint and brushes the next morning.

The best omen for the future of the project is the quality of its planning. In the early stages Mrs. Segal visited many new towns in Europe. At Tapiola in Finland, one of the most widely praised new communities, she snared its founder, Heikki von Hertzen, to serve as a part-time consultant. Gradually she added to the planning team a dozen other firms and individual consultants—specialists in engineering, architecture, environmental design, economics, energy systems, and sociology. Together with the Associates' full-time management staff, small but competent, they have produced an extraordinarily imaginative basic plan. To judge from scale models and the construction already under way, it will be visually exciting, with none of the sterile monotony that deadens so many other large-scale housing enterprises, such as Co-op City in New York. It incorporates novel and apparently farsighted solutions for many urban problems, ranging from the best use of a riverbank to (in Mrs. Segal's phrase) "the psychological effect of planting ten thousand tulip bulbs." Although people like me, who crave a good deal of solitude and open space, might find it claustrophobic, I am sure that for others Cedar-Riverside will be both stimulating and conducive to a sense of community. Mrs. Segal herself believes that its appeal will vary at different stages in a person's life. Single and young married people may especially enjoy its teeming social life. When their children come along, they may prefer to move to Jonathan or some other suburban environment; and when they near retirement, they may want to move back to Cedar-Riverside, for its convenience and cultural assets.

But there are a couple of somber omens too. One of them was the Nixon administration's cutback in 1973 of federal housing and rent-subsidy programs. It probably will not much affect the present stage of the Cedar-Riverside development, for which funding is already committed; but unless new government money begins to flow again within a year or so, the future stages may be hard to finance.

Another was the death in 1973 of Henry McKnight, after a brain tumor operation. His special combination of business and political acumen obviously will be missed; by 1974 I got reports that the Associates were beginning to have managerial and financial problems.

How the project will turn out as a business venture is another open question. Informed outsiders told me that Mrs. Segal's equity is now probably worth something more than $1 million: an adequate, shall we say, rate of growth from her original $19,000 investment eleven years ago. On the other hand, it will be decades—"perhaps not in my lifetime," as she says—before it begins to yield a cash return. What that may be will depend on such imponderables as the occupancy rate and operating costs. So too with the value of the physical investment. If building costs continue to escalate at 12 per cent a year, every brick laid today could look golden in twenty years—provided, of course, that thirty thousand people actually will want to live in Cedar-Riverside when it is completed.

Mrs. Segal gave me the impression that she couldn't care less about how much money she stands to make. Her real reward is the glorious fun she is having right now in building a laboratory for urban living. Its lessons, for good or bad, will begin to flow long before the cash return does.

7.

The Rescue of Jacksonville

The Minnesota experience has provided the best model (in my judgment) for creating the Almost Good Society in one particular kind of metropolitan area. A metropolis, that is, of medium size—say, from 1 million to 3 million people —sprawling over a number of counties, but within the boundaries of a single state. But it is no panacea. Obviously it would not work for a metropolitan area such as New York or St. Louis that laps over into two or more states. Moreover, the Minnesota pattern is not necessarily the best for smaller cities—say, a million people or less—where the entire metropolis is contained within the boundaries of a single big county.

For cities of this description, the best model we have so far was developed in Jacksonville, Florida. As in the case of the Twin Cities, it was born out of crisis: a situation intolerable to most of the people who lived there. And like most of the reforms discussed here, it was fathered by a few men with extraordinary capacities for leadership, who were not themselves professional politicians.

In the early sixties Jacksonville showed all the symptoms of a dying community. Its population was shrinking, as the middle class fled to the suburbs. The 200,000 people left in Jacksonville proper were largely poor, elderly, and black. They were surrounded by some 325,000 suburbanites, who commuted to the city to earn their livings but paid little or nothing for its upkeep. And the city was in an apparently hopeless mess. Its schools had been disaccredited by the Southern Association of Colleges and Schools. Its rivers stank with raw sewage. The business district was decaying, slums kept spreading, and both tax and crime rates were climbing steadily. Air and water supplies were contaminated. Municipal services were shoddy, and getting worse— while the municipal government, riddled with petty corruption, clearly was incapable of doing anything about these woes.

The turning point probably came in 1964. That was the year that scandals were uncovered in the police department, a number of officeholders were indicted, and all fifteen of the city's high schools lost their accreditation. The latter event was a proclamation to the whole country that the school system was no damn good—something that most local residents had long known, but ignored—and that their graduates were not fit for admission to any self-respecting college.

So the oligarchy decided to move. As in many communities in the South (and elsewhere), in Jacksonville a few dozen well-established business and professional men hold a kind of residual power. They have no formal organization, but they see each other frequently at the Seminole, the River, and the University clubs, and the Chamber of Commerce. They devote a good deal of voluntary effort to assorted worthy causes, but almost never run for office or get involved with the grubby toil of day-to-day politics—except in a time of crisis. Some people I talked to suggested that the oligarchs became alarmed in 1964 because the accelerating decay of the city threatened their business interests. No doubt there is some truth in this; but I think they were also motivated by a genuine affection for the community and a sense of civic responsibility. Perhaps, too, they were uncomfortable living in a city they had to be ashamed of.

All of my informants agreed that this group usually looked for leadership to Claude Yates and J. J. Daniel—men of forceful character, considerable wealth, and an intimate knowledge of the community's problems. Yates was the retired general manager of the Southern Bell Telephone and Telegraph Company. Daniel was the head of a highly successful investment and land development firm. The two had been friends for a long while and thought alike on most civic matters.

On January 18, 1965, Yates invited twenty-three acquaintances—oligarchs all—to lunch at the Robert Meyer hotel. They quickly agreed that the time had come not only to throw the rascals out but to junk the whole broken-down machinery of local government. Before the lunch was over, they had drafted the Yates Manifesto: a one-sentence petition to the local delegation to the Florida legislature, asking it to prepare an act that would enable the citizens of Duval County (which contains Jacksonville) to vote on a new scheme of government. The Manifesto made no effort to spell out the details. But it did suggest that all of the governmental bodies—of the county, the city, many special-purpose agencies, and four outlying municipalities within Duval—should be consolidated into a single unit. This marked the beginning of the rebellion. Like the Declaration of Independence in 1776, it was the first public demand for the overthrow of the old system; and like the Declaration, it was drafted not by the poor and oppressed, but by the rich and influential.

The story of the battles that followed has been well told by Richard Martin in his book *Consolidation* (Jacksonville, Crawford Publishing Co., 1968), so there is no need to recount it here. But it may be worthwhile to note some of the lessons that might be of use to other cities in need of reform:

1. *The rebels had strong leadership.* J. J. Daniel became the field commander—the George Washington of the movement—when he was elected chairman of a Study Commission set up by the legislature to design the new scheme of government. As a matter of fact, he looks rather like Washington in his less solemn moments—a big, square-faced man bubbling with energy and high spirits. He gives the impression that he enjoys whatever he is doing, whether planning a new real estate development or fighting a gang of corrupt politicians. He had the advantages of coming from an old and respected Florida family and of being free of any suspicion of personal political ambitions. From his years of voluntary work for the Community Chest, the state university system, and other civic causes, he knew almost everybody of consequence in the community.

As his chief lieutenant he chose Lex Hester, then a thirty-year-old political scientist working in the local office of the U.S. Department of Labor. The two men had never met. Hester wrote a two-page letter applying for the job of executive director of the Commission. It impressed Daniel, and he was further impressed by the comment of a young man in his firm who often played tennis with Hester. He described Hester as "bright, tough, an obsessive worker, with a killer instinct." Precisely the kind of man Daniel needed to run the Commission and to help lead the subsequent fight to get its plan approved by both the state legislature and the local voters.

2. *The reformers involved as many people as possible in their movement from the very beginning.* The Commission's easiest course would have been to hire a few "experts" to draft a blueprint in a back room; but that would have meant almost certain rejection by the voters. Only a community-wide effort, with scores of open hearings and countless meetings of task forces and subcommittees, could accomplish two essential things: (a) to persuade the public of the

need for a really drastic change; and (b) to produce a plan that the voters would both understand and approve. So the proposal that finally emerged was not the Commission's alone; hundreds of private citizens felt that it was *their* plan, because they had helped thrash out its details.

Since Jacksonville had no organization comparable to the Citizens League in Minnesota, the reformers put together an ad hoc group to lead their campaign: Citizens for Better Government. Its speakers' bureau delivered more than two hundred talks within a four-month period.

3. *Their strategy was a bold one.* Instead of trying to patch up and "co-ordinate" the old system, as Miami had done with its scheme of metro government a few years earlier, the reformers opted for an entirely new structure of government.

The Commission's investigations quickly pinpointed the chief troubles of the old system. Although all of Duval County is, in fact, a single metropolitan area, it had never been managed as such. Authority was divided between the city of Jacksonville, four independent municipalities, a county commission, many special-purpose agencies, and the local delegation to the legislature. These separate satrapies could seldom agree on anything; and if they did, they found that nobody really had the power to carry out the decision. Thus the voters never could discover who, if anybody, was responsible for a given failure. Moreover, the central city had most of the problems—from traffic congestion to slums and sewage—but the taxable wealth was mostly located in the suburbs.

So the Commission decided to recommend that this patchwork of weak, overlapping, and confused governments should be abolished out of hand. In its place they called for a single, strong, and simply structured government for the whole county. Authority would be concentrated in an elected city council and a mayor with real power. Most administrative officers would no longer be elected, but appointed by the mayor, so that he could exercise genuine control over the municipal machinery. And the tax burden would be spread fairly over the entire metropolitan area. (Most of the Commission members were suburbanites, and they understood very well that their proposal might increase their own tax bills. They moaned a little, but voted for it anyhow—a fact confusing to true believers in economic determinism.)

Predictably, the entrenched politicians attacked this proposal with a roar of fear and anguish. So did most of the local officeholders who suspected (rightly) that they might lose their jobs or at least get a more demanding boss. For reasons that are still not clear to me, organized labor withheld its support. The plan was even denounced as "communistic"—a quaint notion, in view of its origin.

On the other hand, the blueprint for reform was staunchly supported by the local press. A star reporter, Richard Martin, devoted his whole time to articles explaining it and reporting on the campaign to get it enacted. (He later became historian of the movement and, for a time, director of public relations for the new government.) The churches and nearly all civic organizations lined up behind the plan.

So, surprisingly, did most of the black community. In several other metropolitan areas, Negroes have resisted consolidation efforts, suspecting them as a device to weaken black voting power in the inner city, to the advantage of white suburbanites. But in Jacksonville the black leaders were sophisticated enough to realize that their needs—decent schools, housing, and jobs—could never be satisfied under the old system.

One of these leaders was Earl Johnson, who had fought

hard in the civil rights wars as lawyer for the National Association for the Advancement of Colored People. He told me that the blacks might well have taken over the government of the old city within a few years as white voters continued to move out.

"But what good would that have done us?" he said. "We would just have been receivers in bankruptcy."*

The critical event of the fight occurred in the spring of 1967, when Hans Tanzler decided to run as a reform candidate for mayor. He was a judge of unquestioned integrity, and he had the political charisma of a Kennedy. A onetime star athlete, he is tall, handsome, and oozing with southern charm. The ladies loved him, and the men were impressed by his sincerity—and his demonstrated competence as a lawyer and civic activist.

While the Study Commission's reform plan was still under fierce debate, Tanzler won the mayoralty and carried a slate of other reform candidates into office with him. During his campaign he had remained noncommittal about city-county consolidation; but soon after taking office he endorsed it as "a giant step forward." That did it.

Weeks of maneuvering and infighting still lay ahead, to win the approval of the legislature. In the process some compromises had to be made. The proposed authority for the mayor was whittled down a little; limits were placed on future tax rates; and the outlying municipalities were granted a considerable degree of autonomy. But the essentials of the new charter came through intact. And on August

* Johnson was elected a councilman as soon as the new government was established and primarily by white votes since he is one of the five chosen at-large. Of the fourteen other councilmen who were elected by districts, two were black. In the beginning there was a good deal of mutual coolness between them and their white colleagues; but within a year blacks and whites were, by all accounts, working together cordially and effectively.

8, 1967, the consolidation proposal was approved in a countywide referendum by a majority of almost 2 to 1.

The victory was unique. No other American community had succeeded in this century in remodeling its government so completely, and at the first try. (A somewhat similar reform had been defeated when first proposed in Nashville, Tennessee, but got adopted in a second election in 1962.) Since 1967, seven other county-city mergers have been accomplished, following the Jacksonville example: Columbus, Georgia; Carson City, Nevada; Juneau and Sitka, Alaska; Indianapolis, Indiana; Suffolk, Virginia; and Lexington, Kentucky. Only seven.

But a good many other communities are likely to begin to explore this road as soon as the news gets around about the results in Jacksonville. For the new Tanzler administration—armed with authority to act, and with reorganized executive departments to carry out its decisions—began to mop up its inherited messes with almost manic energy.

Its most dramatic accomplishment was the cleaning up of the county's polluted air and waterways. Previous administrations, afflicted with the old Confederate distrust of the feds, had not even asked for their share of the Washington money available for this and other purposes. Tanzler got every penny he could lay his hands on, plus whatever state money was going; and he raised some more through water and sewer charges and a $131-million bond issue. With these funds the administration began buying up private utility companies that had been ill-serving the metropolitan area and unified them into a single efficient system. (Socialism, yet!) In addition, it started replacing more than a hundred miles of crumbling sewer lines, expanded the old treatment plants and started new ones, and cracked down on industries polluting both air and water. Result: raw sewage is no longer dumped into the St. Johns River. And you can now breathe in Jacksonville without choking.

The schools were quickly upgraded and regained their accreditation.

Fire protection was improved so markedly that insurance rates came down.

Ten new health centers were built, and mobile clinics began to take medical services to outlying areas.

More than 16,500 streetlights were installed and many streets were repaved, especially in the poorer—that is, the black—sections of town.

New parks, swimming pools, and recreation centers are going up all over the place. Incidentally, Jacksonville is one of the few American cities that have used their waterfronts to good advantage; its parks, boat ramps, and civic buildings look positively dazzling to anyone used to the crumbling piers and warehouses of New York.

Merging of the old county and city police forces, with their conflicting jurisdictions and inadequate personnel and equipment, has considerably improved the safety of the city. And it saved a lot of money—nearly half a million on patrol cars alone.

For the first time the Planning Board is able to make coherent plans for the development of the whole metropolitan area—840 square miles, which makes it the second biggest American city in acreage. (Juneau, since its consolidation, is the largest: 3,108 square miles, most of them empty.)

As a result of the economies achieved by merging duplicate city and county agencies, and the modernization of the tax system, the new government has been able to lower property taxes for five consecutive years—from $51 per thousand dollars' valuation in 1967 to $29 in 1971. And if you compare the total burden of all taxes—property, sales, income, and automobile levies—in the thirty largest American cities, Jacksonville's is the lowest of all. (Boston's taxes are the highest. A family of four, earning $25,000 a year, paid a total of $668 in 1973 in Jacksonville; in Boston, the same kind of family paid $3,314).*

Jacksonville is no longer a dying city. Because it is rapidly becoming a more attractive place to live and work, new industries are moving in fast. Ten new plants, providing three thousand jobs, have been located in an industrial park built on an abandoned airport. Office buildings—including a thirty-five-story insurance company headquarters—are going up in the once-decaying downtown district. The most heartening news of all was the announcement in 1972 that Tenneco and Westinghouse Electric had selected Jacksonville as the site for a joint venture in building offshore atomic power plants. The manufacturing complex will cost about $350 million and is expected to employ more than twelve thousand people.

All this has led to a marked relaxation of racial bitterness. Whites and blacks no longer have to compete so fiercely for scarce jobs. Negroes now see their own people in positions of consequence—the city council, a federal magistracy, all local banks, and every city department. What is probably more important, Jacksonville blacks are now getting satisfaction of some age-old grievances—bad schools, unpaved and unlighted streets, a shortage of decent low-rent housing, inadequate public health service, poor garbage collection, and cheating storekeepers. (The city's new consumers' ser-

---

* These figures come from a 1973 study by the District of Columbia Department of Finance and Revenue, "Major State and Local Tax Burdens in Washington Compared with Those in the 30 Largest Cities." Washington, incidentally, fell exactly in the middle of the list.

In fairness, however, it should be noted that Jacksonville is now collecting about $5 million a year in sewage fees imposed since the consolidation, and its water fees have about doubled. Although some of the other Big Thirty cities do not levy such charges, the sums involved are not large enough to invalidate the comparison.

vice handles more than 1,100 complaints a month.) A Community Relations Commission is working on a dozen projects, from the feeding of eleven thousand disadvantaged children during summer months to job training and placement of blacks in executive careers.

This does not mean, of course, that Jacksonville has reached the apotheosis of racial justice. Blacks are still concentrated mostly in the slums of the old city—about 45 per cent of its population—and because there is no satisfactory mass transit system, they find it hard to commute to new jobs in the outlying parts of Duval County. Earl Johnson summed up the situation like this: "We still have a long way to go, but we have come a long way too. The white members of the city council have learned a lot since consolidation. The black members have taught them to feel some empathy for the poor."

Johnson himself has come a long way. When I first met him, he had just moved his family into an attractive home in the aptly named Mandarin district of Jacksonville, one of the choice and, until then, all-white neighborhoods.

"We didn't expect any active hostility," he said. "I did think we probably would be ignored—you know, kind of invisible—for quite a while. But I wasn't looking for what actually happened.

"While we were getting the furniture moved in, a big Cadillac drove up in front of the house and the chauffeur got out with a tray of white camellias. It was a present from a lady up the street who wanted to welcome us to the neighborhood. Then later that day the man next door walked over to help me fix up the filter of our swimming pool.

"Our relationships with the neighbors have been more than good—I would have to say excellent. The only criticism I've heard has been from some of my black friends, who claim I copped out by moving away from the downtown section."

Since about 1970, Mayor Tanzler—who apparently can get re-elected for as long as he wants the job—has been getting more out-of-town lecture invitations than he can accept. But he does like to spread the gospel whenever he can by speaking before meetings of municipal officials. At one such conference in Atlanta, I heard him begin his talk by saying:

"I don't give a damn whether you adopt consolidation governments for your cities or not. It doesn't mean a cent to me. I don't get any commission for selling the idea. So if you want to go ahead wasting your money and running a bunch of second-rate communities, that's all right with me. But if you are ready for something better, let me tell you what we've done in Jacksonville. . . ."

By the end of the hour he had a room full of converts—and I suspect that his message did not stop with them.

The Seattle Vigilantes

One of the most influential men in the state of Washington has never held public office and never expects to. He is not rich. He does not move in the local high society, such as it is: in fact, his social life is pretty close to nil. He does not command any political machine, ethnic group, corporation, newspaper, or broadcasting system. In sum, he is a walking contradiction of everything C. Wright Mills used to tell us about the power elite.

Nevertheless James R. Ellis is largely responsible for much that has happened in the state's public life during the last twenty years. A Seattle politician described him to me, only half-jokingly, as "our homegrown Pericles"—and he is, indeed, reshaping Seattle almost as drastically as Pericles reshaped Athens in the fifth century B.C. But his methods are different. After much wearisome trial and error, Ellis discovered that in the peculiar political climate of Washington he can best get things done by working outside the regular channels of government. Accordingly he has made himself the unofficial leader of a kind of modern-day vigilante movement, taking on the rough jobs that elected politicians are unable (or unwilling) to tackle. As a consequence, the patterns emerging in Washington are markedly different from those we have noted in Jacksonville, Minneapolis, and elsewhere.

Ellis would seem to be an unlikely man for this role. He is

a lawyer who specializes in the unglamorous business of municipal finance—a middle-aged man of middling build with nothing colorful about his dress or personality. He is not in the best of health, suffering from incipient ulcers and chronic fatigue. If he possesses charisma—supposedly an indispensable item of equipment for public leaders these days—I have never been able to detect it. He speaks in a quiet, unemphatic voice, completely lacking the dramatic flourishes of a Hans Tanzler. Yet he has the knack of setting forth his ideas with clarity and a curious sort of understated conviction. After listening to him for a couple of hours during our first meeting in 1968, I began to understand why his word carries so much weight in his community. He is, simply, a hard man to disbelieve.

This was not always so. For a good many years Ellis was not only a prophet without honor in his own country, but a prophet without an audience.

He went into the prophet business in 1951 when he was a hungry young attorney only two years out of law school. He and his family lived in a log cabin up in the mountains east of Seattle—partly because it was cheap, but mostly because they all loved the casual out-of-doors life that always has been one of the enchantments of the Pacific Northwest. In that year he began to suspect that this way of life was in jeopardy, not only for the Ellis family, but for everybody living within fifty miles or so of Puget Sound.

"I guess you could say that I became a premature member of the ecology movement," Ellis told me. "Nobody had heard of ecology in those days, and my friends thought I was some kind of nut."

For he had realized, sooner than almost anybody else, that the whole area was about to be swamped by a wave of new industry and new people. Like Jeremiah, he started to preach the woes to come.

Seattle wasn't ready to cope with the imminent invasion. It had no plans for the rational location of new factories, or for housing their workers, moving their traffic, or even taking care of their sewage. Worse yet, nobody had any responsibility for making such plans. The likely result was that the entire countryside between the Sound and the mountains—one of the spectacularly lovely sites of this continent—would become a shapeless, smog-choked urban nightmare like Los Angeles.

Hardly anybody listened. Seattle was then an easygoing lumber and fishing port where nothing very dramatic had happened for the last hundred years. It was hard to believe that a boom—touched off by the Korean war and the rapid expansion of Boeing and related industries—would soon make it one of the fastest-growing metropolitan areas in America. Only a few genteel ladies in the League of Women Voters and the Good Government buffs of the Municipal League—generally regarded as a bunch of harmless eccentrics—paid much attention to Ellis's predictions. (Some real estate speculators listened too; but orderly, controlled growth was the last thing in the world they wanted.)

Nevertheless, Ellis was young and brash enough to think that he understood not only the problem, but what to do about it. He took a leave of absence from his law firm to help draft a new charter for King County—a new scheme of government that would give the county at least part of the authority it needed to direct the future growth of Seattle and the smaller communities within its borders. It had the enthusiastic backing of the two leagues, but that wasn't enough. When the proposal was put to a vote in 1952, it was overwhelmingly defeated.

By this time Ellis was broke; at one point when he was working as a volunteer on the charter-reform project, his bank balance was down to $22. So he went back to his law practice to recoup—and to try to figure out a new scheme of metropolitan government that might attract wider public support. He kept preaching too, wherever he could get a handful of people to listen. One by one, he enlisted a little corps of disciples, including not only the Good Government amateurs but also for the first time a few idealistic young politicians in both parties. (One of them was Dan Evans, then a freshman legislator, later governor of Washington— one of the most effective of the liberal Republicans.)

In a long and brilliant campaign of persuasion, this band of political guerrillas sold the legislature on a new design for a limited metropolitan government, empowered to deal with such matters as sewage disposal, public transportation, and area-wide planning. Again it went before the voters—and again, in a 1958 referendum, it was defeated.

Nobody could have blamed Ellis, after seven years of apparently fruitless labor, if he had decided that the cause was hopeless and that he had better turn his energies to making money and playing golf. Instead he decided that maybe he had been on the wrong track all along. Obviously the people of Seattle weren't going to buy a supergovernment, no matter how it was packaged. They were then—and still are today—besotted with anachronistic frontier traditions. Many of them distrust all politicians, bureaucrats, and forms of government; and the bigger the government, the more their suspicions bristle. Their innate political philosophy (so far as I can tell) often seems to be an improbable blend of Jeffersonian democracy, hard-shell conservatism, and anarchy.

But they are nevertheless willing, now and then, to tackle a single dramatic project with the co-operative enthusiasm that once went into frontier barn raisings. Conceivably that kind of spirit might be mobilized, Ellis thought, to attack the region's problems one at a time.

"The obvious place to start," Ellis said, "was with our sewage problem."

(Familar words. Since the late fifties, in city after city I found that a sewage problem had served as the detonator that set off a series of changes in government.)

Seattle lies between two magnificent bodies of water: Puget Sound to the west and twenty-four-mile-long Lake Washington to the east. Both offered lovely homesites, unsurpassed possibilities for recreation—and a cheap, convenient place to dump sewage. By the mid-fifties those homesites were no longer so attractive, many beaches had been closed, and Lake Washington seemed doomed to become a "dead" body of water like Lake Erie. Also, it stank.

"From our standpoint," Ellis said, "it probably helped that the summer of 1958 was a hot one. The lake got pretty bad that year and even some of the people who had fought us came around to agreeing that something had to be done."

So he rallied his vigilantes once more and came up with yet another proposal: a $135-million sewerage system to serve the entire metropolitan area, 231 square miles containing 800,000 people, in fourteen cities and towns. This time, for a change, they won. The enabling act—drafted on Ellis's dining room table—passed the legislature handily, and in September of 1958 the Metro sanitation plan was approved by referendum. During the next ten years, it proved to be a spectacular success. Lake Washington was saved, in the nick of time, and Puget Sound is now cleaner than it has been in the last 150 years.

The moral seemed plain enough: the barn-raising technique is the best—sometimes the only—way to get things done in that part of the country.

With that lesson in mind, another group of citizens—led this time by Ed Carlson, Seattle's leading hotel man, and a lawyer named Joe Gandy—began to dream of a gaudier kind of barn: a World's Fair, no less. It seemed to fit the specifications for a successful civic undertaking, as demonstrated by Ellis's laborious decade of trial and error. It would be a single, short-term project. It could be handled outside of the humdrum (and suspect) channels of government. It would arouse no partisan animosities. And it might be dramatic enough to enlist the volunteer efforts of hundreds of talented people.

One of the most energetic of these volunteers was Dewayne Kreager, a management consultant. "We really had no business trying to put on a World's Fair," he told me. "Seattle wasn't supposed to be big-league enough for that kind of operation. Besides, everybody knew it would be a financial disaster, as such ventures nearly always are. But we were just cocky and ignorant enough to give it a try."

The result astonished everybody, including such metabolic optimists as Kreager. The 1962 Fair not only proved a critical success and a bonanza for Seattle's businessmen and hotelkeepers; it also ended up—unbelievably—with a cash surplus. And because its main buildings had been cunningly designed to serve a double purpose, it left Seattle with a $90-million cultural center which didn't cost the taxpayer a nickel.

Another, and more important, legacy was intangible. When the Fair closed, the whole civic leadership of the community was exhausted, triumphant—and convinced that they could accomplish almost anything they set their minds to. Scores of able men and women—many of them previously strangers to each other—had enjoyed the heady experience of working together in a common cause. Nobody planned it that way, but in retrospect it seems plain that the Fair prepared the ground for Jim Ellis's most daring foray to date.

He waited until the sweat had dried on the community's collective brow; and then on November 3, 1965, in a now famous speech before the Seattle Rotary Club, he summoned his followers to another breathtakingly ambitious undertaking. Its purpose was to accomplish most of the things which he had once hoped to do through a metropolitan government—but without setting up such a government. Instead he proposed that a group of unofficial volunteers should get together to draw up a plan for the future of Greater Seattle—a plan that would anticipate a doubling of the population by 1986. To put it into effect, he suggested a massive capital investment in a rapid-transit system, parks and open spaces, highway and sewer improvements, and the other key facilities the future metropolis would have to have.

The investment would be made through the existing city, town, and county governments in the Puget Sound area. But the volunteer group would see to it that all the pieces fitted together into a coherent whole. The resulting framework would, God willing, direct the future growth of the area into an orderly, shapely, and livable community for two million people. And the framework had better be laid right now; for, if not, the specter of "Los Angelization" was just over the horizon.

This notion, which Ellis christened the Forward Thrust program, caught on immediately. One reason was that it followed the pattern—a one-shot convulsive effort by a temporary, unofficial organization—that had worked so well with the Metro sewerage project and the World's Fair. But equally important was the fact that the power structure of the state had learned to trust Ellis. By this time, virtually everybody was convinced that his sole motivation was the public welfare. If he had ever shown a trace of personal political ambition, his influence would have evaporated overnight; but since he never had, no politician in either party feared him as a potential rival, and even the most conservative industrialists no longer suspected him of being a socialist crackpot.

Consequently he was able to enlist for his Forward Thrust committee, or posse, an extraordinary array of talent. The original two hundred members included many of the region's leading businessmen, lawyers, professors from the University of Washington, public servants, clergymen, conservationists, and energetic do-gooders. (Labor and Negro organizations, as it turned out, were probably underrepresented—not deliberately, but because some of their ablest leaders were too busy, or unwilling, to take on the assignment.) The committee raised money for an office and small staff, much of it from the members' own pockets. But the main contribution was hard work—thousands of man-hours devoted to systematic study of the region's needs, problems, and priorities.

The end product, after two years of labor and argument, was a bundle of interlocking proposals for capital investment. The price tag added up to $819 million—the biggest single improvement program, so far as I can discover, ever attempted at one time by any American metropolis. Before it could be laid before the voters, the legislature had to pass eighteen enabling acts; under the prodding of Governor Evans, political leaders of both parties, and the Seattle business community, it finally did so—after a good deal of nervous debate. (The rural legislators, especially, were appalled by the thought of anybody spending that kind of money.)

Meanwhile the Forward Thrusters were carrying on a masterly campaign of voter education—or, as their opponents preferred to call it, propaganda. These critics apparently were few and not very effective. Right up until the final weeks before the election, public opinion polls indicated that the whole package probably would be approved by a comfortable majority.

The package consisted of twelve separate bond issues—

six of them to be obligations of King County, five of them to be obligations of the city of Seattle, and one to be an obligation of the Metro-district which already was responsible for the regional sewerage system. This last was, at least in Ellis's eyes, by all odds the most important. It called for $385 million—to be matched by twice that much in federal funds—to build a rapid-transit system, which would be constructed and managed by the same Metro organization that had coped with the sanitation problem so competently. Under the state constitution, each of the twelve proposals had to be approved by at least 60 per cent of the votes cast.

When the ballots were finally counted, on the evening of February 13, 1968, the transit proposal was beaten—although it did manage to get a trifle more than 50 per cent of the votes. Four other bond issues were defeated along with it, one of them (for a storm-water-control system) losing by only a fraction of 1 per cent.

"It was a heartbreaker, all right," Ellis told me. "So many good people had worked so hard, and with such high hopes. But after we got over our first disappointment, we began to see that we actually had won a considerable victory. After all, the voters did approve $118 million for parks and recreation—enough to give Seattle the most magnificent park system in the world. And we got some other key items, too. For example, a stadium that can accommodate big-league sports clubs, and a youth service center, and some big improvements in highways and fire protection and blighted neighborhoods. Besides, the ball game isn't over yet."

What he meant was that he planned another Forward Thrust campaign to focus on rapid transit alone—something he believed indispensable for the salvation of Seattle. This too ended in defeat—thanks to a temporary depression in the aircraft industry and the combined opposition of the highway lobby, road contractors, and taxpayers who were afraid of another big bond issue.

Was Ellis downhearted? Indeed he was. But he was not yet ready to give up. By 1971 he and the other transit advocates had come up with a revised plan, based on buses rather than rails and considerably less expensive. To avoid a bond issue, it would be financed by a sales tax, plus state and federal contributions and its own fare revenues. New leadership was enlisted, notably State Senator Joel Pritchard (later elected to Congress); Aubrey Davis, mayor of the suburban community of Mercer Island and chairman of the Metro transit; and Harvey Poll, a lawyer and veteran of the anti-pollution movement.

Almost unbelievably, this time the vigilantes won. After fifteen years of discouragement, six battles in the legislature, and five elections, the voters both of Seattle and of the outlying areas of King County finally approved a scheme for mass transit.

Most significant of all was the nature of the plan. It did not call for another special-purpose agency, which would have fragmented the pattern of government still further. Instead it placed the management of transit under the existing Metro organization. At the same time, it expanded the boundaries of Metro to cover all of King County—virtually the entire metropolitan commuting area, containing twenty-six cities with a population totaling 1,100,000.

Thus Metro became a multi-purpose agency. In addition to sewage and public transport, it is capable of taking on still more jobs whenever the voters so decide, for example, comprehensive planning for the region, water supply, garbage disposal, and parks—the additional functions envisaged by Ellis when he drafted that first, unsuccessful proposal for metropolitan government back in 1952. If it does evolve in this direction, it might eventually end up looking very much like the Twin Cities Metropolitan Council. Alternatively, someday Metro might be merged with the governments of

Seattle and King County, roughly according to the Jacksonville pattern.

Something of the kind, I believe, is bound to happen sooner or later. Granted that Ellis & Cohorts have passed some pretty good miracles—but he won't last forever. The techniques he has developed will continue to serve only if he is succeeded by other civic leaders equally dedicated, untainted by political ambition, and adroit at mobilizing volunteers. That is asking a lot of any community. One Ellis in a generation is about all any city can reasonably hope to produce.

Besides, even with such leadership, I suspect that the neo-vigilante system is incapable of handling the really controversial problems of government. It depends on a broad and fragile consensus—the sort that can be put together only to support uplift and civic improvement projects that nobody but a Scrooge would publicly oppose. But if faced with a sharply divisive issue, such as tax reform or the location of low-income housing, it would surely break down. Moreover, you can't really run a modern metropolis by a series of spasmodic efforts, however impressive each one of them may be. Forward Thrust did produce an astonishingly well-integrated plan, considering that it was put together by amateurs in their spare time;* and it did carry out major parts of that plan by means of a one-time massive capital investment. But all this is no substitute for metropolitan planning as a continuous, long-range process, by some agency with authority to resolve conflicts and enforce its decisions.

* They did get a good deal of professional help from the staff of the Puget Sound Governmental Conference, mentioned earlier as one of the most effective of the Councils of Governments. Its jurisdiction covers the four counties bordering the Sound, the twenty-nine cities and towns within their borders, and two Indian tribal councils. More recently, its studies of population, traffic flow, and growth trends provided much of the groundwork for the transit plan.

Nevertheless, for cities in other parts of the country, the Seattle experience offers a few encouraging lessons:

The Forward Thrust technique is one way to deal with an environmental emergency when the community is not yet ready for a real metropolitan government.

It can enlist talents and energies that a regular governmental agency probably could not muster.

It can serve—maybe—as a step toward something better.

It demonstrates what one man can accomplish, armed with nothing but an idea and unlimited persistence.

A Washington politician who has often disagreed with Ellis put it this way:

"Hell, anybody could do what Jim Ellis did. All you have to do is work your ass off for twenty years without pay."

When Hercules did that in the Greece of long ago, he was called a hero. But we, of course, live in an age that doesn't believe in heroes.

9.

New Towns and the Old Ideas of Henry George

One evening in the spring of 1937, I was having a drink in the lounge car of a Washington-to-New York train when the Honorable John Taber sat down beside me. He was an elderly Congressman from Auburn, New York, a Republican of chrome-steel conservatism, whom I had gotten to know when I was covering the Capitol for the Associated Press.

"Do you know what that madman Roosevelt is up to now?" he said, for openers. "He is building a new town just north of Washington. I have confidential information that he plans to hide an arsenal of rifles and machine guns there, and to assemble a mob of revolutionaries from all over the country. When he is ready, he will order them to march on the Capitol and disband Congress. He calls the place Greenbelt."

I told him that I did indeed know about Greenbelt, because I had recently become a minor member of the Resettlement Administration staff that was building it. We did have a revolutionary purpose all right, but not the sort he had in mind. We were going to revolutionize the urban environment. We hoped to demonstrate a better way for people to live—in low-cost but comfortable homes, in a parklike setting free of automobile traffic, within walking distance of their work, and surrounded by a greenbelt of fields and forests. An idyllic place, where the deserving poor could move from the slums of Washington and Baltimore. A model, moreover, for the rest of the country—and to make the lesson triply plain, we were building two more greenbelt towns near Cincinnati and Milwaukee. Eventually we expected to see hundreds of communities like them springing up all over America.

The Honorable John gobbled like a turkey and got so red in the face that I thought (hopefully) he might have a stroke. When he regained his voice, he announced that our scheme was, if anything, worse than building a hideout for an armed mob.

"Don't you realize," he said, "that you are undermining our whole system of capitalistic free enterprise?"

As it turned out, he needn't have worried. The Resettlement Administration's experiment with new towns never amounted to much. Because they were built largely by unskilled workers on relief, they were not actually low-cost. In those depression days it proved impossible to bring in industries to employ the town's residents. Idealistic efforts to set up co-operative ownership of the projects, along with co-op stores and services, ended in failure. Eventually the houses were sold to their tenants or on the open market, and the greenbelts fell into the hands of real estate operators. The towns became, in effect, just three more suburban communities—better planned than most, but not radically different from the subdivisions and tract developments sprawling around all of our big cities. Some of their features—the superblock site plan and the separation of car and foot traffic—were later picked up by some of the more imaginative real estate developers. But the greenbelt town experiment did not really revolutionize anything.

The reason was that we idealists of the Resettlement Administration did not even recognize the truly revolutionary potential of new towns. We focused entirely on their physical aspect: the design of a better environment. That was a laudable goal, but hardly a fresh one. Intellectually it was no advance beyond the ideas set forth in 1898 by Ebenezer Howard in his *Garden Cities of Tomorrow*, the Old Testament of town planning. What we overlooked were the ideas that another reformer (and friend of Howard's) was generating at about the same time: the principles Henry George set forth in his *Progress and Poverty*.

For the really radical possibilities in new towns are not physical but fiscal. They offer a means of tapping a huge new source of revenue by capturing for the public some of the billions that traditionally have gone into the pockets of land speculators.

Ever since George Washington's day, land speculation has been the favorite American way of getting rich. To be sure, those who tried it did not call themselves speculators; they were shrewd investors, or farsighted believers in the American future. The trick was to guess the direction in which an ever-growing population would flow, and then buy up cheap land in its path. If you guessed wrong (as Washington sometimes did) or bought too soon (as Squire Hawkins did in *The Gilded Age*) you would lose your investment. But if you were lucky enough to guess right, as John Jacob Astor did, you could sit back in your easy chair and watch your land rise in value day by day. You didn't have to do a thing; "natural growth" would work for you like Midas's golden touch.

Actually, of course, "natural" is the wrong word because urban land values are a manufactured article. They are created largely through public investment—in highways, water supply, sewers, parks, and all the other necessities of civilization. The taxpayer foots the bill, and the land speculator takes the profit.

For example, New York taxpayers spent $350 million to build the Verrazano Bridge across the Narrows to Staten Island. Almost overnight the island's landowners found their property values had increased by a total of $700 million. When Toronto built its rapid-transit system, the price of land near the new subway stations went up as much as tenfold. The location of an interchange on a national highway is a decision that can make millions for the surprised farmers bordering the site because their pastures will soon be covered with motels, filling stations, truck depots, and condominiums. The Great American Money Machine has always worked this way since the building of the first turnpikes, canals, and railways at public expense. That is why old Henry George thought that a single tax on rising land values would not only finance these public improvements, but cover all the other costs of government. Nobody paid any attention to him, of course; too many of us had a vested interest, or hope, in rising land values. (I have myself. I happen to own a few acres on a once-remote bay on Long Island Sound. Since Interstate 95 made this stretch of coast accessible, the land's value has trebled.)

The only trouble with the Money Machine is its unpredictability. Even the canniest speculator can't always guess where, or when, that bridge or interchange or subway station will be built, or in which direction a metropolis is likely to grow. Some of the uncertainty can be removed by bribing legislators or highway engineers; but that mode of operation has risks of its own.

In the years after World War II, when the housing shortage was desperate, it occurred to a number of businessmen that they could eliminate the uncertainty in another way: by directing urban growth themselves instead of trying to anticipate the whims of government and the market. In principle, the operation is simple. You buy up a few thousand acres of vacant land and build homes, stores, theaters, schools, churches, and office buildings. You persuade a few industrial firms to locate factories there. You take whatever subsidies you can get in the form of loan guarantees, Federal Housing Administration mortgages, highway construction, school funds, and the like. And in the end, you sell off the land to the residents at ten—or a hundred—times as much as you paid for it. For if the new community is well planned, it will be an irresistibly attractive place to live. No commuting. No slums. No smog, or traffic jams, or the nerve-shattering noise of the city. A semi-rural idyll, in fact, much like the Resettlement people had hoped to create at Greenbelt.

Old John Taber would never have believed that such a socialistic idea could be adopted by the capitalistic free enterprise system. Yet by the mid-sixties a score of major corporations had plunged into the new town business— among them, Connecticut General Life Insurance, Gulf Oil, Goodyear Tire and Rubber, ITT, and the Walt Disney organization. By the end of the decade, more than a hundred so-called "new towns" were a-building. Most of these did not, in fact, deserve the name: they were merely outsized suburban developments, or retirement villages, or vacation home colonies—with no industry and a bare minimum of community and cultural facilities. But about twenty were designed as genuine new towns. That is, they would have a minimum population of at least thirty thousand; they would provide job opportunities within their boundaries for a good many of their residents; and they would include all the ingredients—from office buildings to coffee shops and theaters—for civilized living.

In practice, the private development of such a community turned out to be anything but simple.

To begin with, the assembly of a big acreage at a reasonable price—no more than $1,500 an acre, as a rough rule of thumb—is a tricky business. To get the 17,800 acres he needed for Columbia, the best known of the new towns, James Rouse had to create an underground organization that moved with secrecy and deviousness worthy of the CIA. Buying under many guises, it acquired 164 farms within nine months—about a tenth of the entire area of Howard County, Maryland. In spite of all security precautions, however, these purchases rapidly pushed up the price of the land he wanted from $300 to $3,000 an acre. Additional purchases five years later raised his total investment in land alone to $44 million—an average cost of nearly $2,500 an acre, which some financiers consider dangerously high. But in view of its situation—just between the fast-growing metropolises of Washington and Baltimore—Rouse feels he got a bargain. Indeed, it is doubtful whether a private developer can ever again assemble such a tract, in an equally strategic location, anywhere within the densely settled northeastern states.

Consequently, most of the new towns have been started in the West and South, where land comes in bigger and cheaper pieces. Using tactics much like Rouse's, the Disney organization picked up 27,000 acres in central Florida for about $200 an acre—the site for Walt Disney World and eventually for something to be called the Experimental Prototype Community of Tomorrow. The most profitable of the new communities may turn out to be Irvine, just south of Los Angeles. It is going up on the 88,000 acres of a ranch assembled more than a century ago by James Irvine and held by his descendants ever since. His cost has been estimated at about thirty-five cents an acre; some of this land has been sold recently for more than $300,000 an acre, and prices probably will continue to climb as the new city approaches its ultimate population of half a million. But such a project, like Columbia, will be difficult if not impossible to duplicate.

A second difficulty of the new town builders is the mind-boggling size of the investments they have to make. Rouse and his associates—principally Connecticut General Life Insurance, Teachers Insurance and Annuity Association, and the Chase Manhattan Bank—have sunk about $100 million into Columbia. Reston has cost its backers at least $85 million; and the Disney organization put $400 million into its Florida venture, with more to come—probably much more—before its Community of Tomorrow is completed. Such sums are necessary, not only for the land, but for the streets, sewerage systems, water supply, and community facilities that have to be built before a dime can be recovered by the resale of properties to the new residents.

Moreover, this has to be "patient money," as Jim Rouse puts it. Unlike the small speculative builder, who hopes to turn his capital over every year or two, the investors in a new town cannot expect to get their money back for decades. Rouse started buying land for Columbia in 1962. At this writing, he hopes to regain his investment, with a profit, by 1981, when the community should reach its optimum population of 110,000. Meanwhile, the Rouse Company pays no dividends. The insurance companies that went into the deal with him are collecting steady interest, but they too will have to wait a long time before they realize any capital gains.

Obviously such "patient money" in gigantic blocks will always be hard to find. Robert E. Simon, Jr., couldn't do it. He started to build Reston, Virginia—the other new town in the Washington area—with his own money, before lining up really large-scale financing. Moreover, he failed to do the meticulous economic forecasting that has always characterized Rouse's operations. Simon not only did not know where most of the capital would come from; neither did he know precisely how much he would need, or when and how it could be repaid. Result: he sank $1,800,000 of his own cash into the project before he lost control of it to Gulf Oil and the John Hancock insurance company. When, and whether, their investment will turn a profit is still an open question.

A third difficulty is political. A privately sponsored new town is mortally dependent on the good will of the local governments—usually several of them—which must grant the necessary changes in zoning and building codes. If they are unco-operative they can halt the project altogether, even after the land is assembled. If they are merely dubious, they may delay operations for months or years—possibly a worse fate because interest charges on the original investment keep piling up at a murderous rate. For this reason, as Rouse points out, "Timing is the essence. You have to keep moving fast."

Consequently, the promoter has to have extraordinary political talents. He must be an evangelist (like Rouse and Gloria Segal) with enough eloquence to sell his vision to thousands of skeptics in the area affected by his project. How Rouse did this, speaking day and night to any group in Howard County that would listen to him, is a fascinating story in itself; it is told in detail in Gurney Breckenfeld's *Columbia and the New Cities*, the best book that I have found in all the voluminous literature on the subject.*

People who combine such political skill with financial acumen, vision, a talent for large-scale planning, and the ability to manage an undertaking of great complexity are rare indeed. Rouse, I suspect, is unique—the nearest thing to a genius that the new town business has yet produced. In some ways he reminds me of Jim Ellis: so ordinary in

* I am indebted to Breckenfeld for some of the figures cited earlier in this chapter.

appearance and demeanor that he would look right at home in a shoe clerks' convention. Yet, like Ellis, when he begins to talk, his fervor is irresistible. He hopes to make a great deal of money out of Columbia simply to prove that it can be done. A whopping profit would be the surest way of luring other entrepreneurs into new town building. But in money per se he has almost no interest; he would, I am sure, continue to live simply and work fourteen hours a day no matter how many millions he might have in the bank. What really motivates him is the same thing that motivated the New Dealers who built the greenbelt towns: a passion to demonstrate a better environment for urban living.

He will succeed, I think, where we failed. Already he has accomplished much of what he wanted. By 1973 Columbia, with thirty thousand residents, was a full-fledged community and a remarkably attractive one. If I were free to move, I would rather live there than any place I know. Its architecture is generally undistinguished—far less imaginative than that of Reston—but the setting is superb. Rouse has indeed kept the promise he had made in his original announcement: to "set the highest possible standards of beauty, safety, and convenience . . . providing major areas of permanent open space, lakes, parks, and scenery." He also has succeeded far better than most new town builders in enticing industries: about seventy of them by 1973, including a General Electric plant that eventually will employ twelve thousand people. And the community does have, as promised, a wide range of cultural and recreational facilities, from pubs to Dag Hammarskjöld College.

I don't really understand the bookkeeping of the Rouse Company, which is engaged in many enterprises in addition to Columbia. Nor can I tell from the published reports how well the town itself is doing financially. But friends who are far wiser than I am in such matters and who have studied the Columbia financial projects in detail think it quite probable that Rouse will succeed in his secondary ambition: to come out with an impressive profit by the early eighties.

Nevertheless, I doubt whether this will produce the result he hopes for: that is, to encourage the private building of many other new communities throughout the country. No doubt some will be attempted from time to time where circumstances are especially favorable—as in the case of Flower Mound New Town, designed for sixty-five thousand occupants near Fort Worth and Dallas, or St. Charles Communities, in southern Maryland, where eighty thousand people may be living by 1993. But in many places where housing is most urgently needed, the job is just too daunting for private enterprisers. Bringing together the land, the capital, the necessary political decisions, and the array of specialized talent—all on an inexorably tight schedule—is an undertaking as complex (and risky) as a flight to the moon.

Finally, a privately developed new town does not necessarily result in public benefits. Most of those that I know about are, indeed, preferable to the most likely alternative: that is, an endless repetition of the piecemeal tract developments that already disfigure so much of our suburban landscape. But unless the developer is (like Rouse) dedicated to enhancing the environment and willing to sacrifice some profit to do so, a new town can turn out to be an ecological disaster. An example is the Palm Coast development now being built by ITT on a 92,000-acre site about twenty miles south of St. Augustine, Florida. Evidently the corporation's purpose here is simply to reap the biggest possible profit in the shortest possible time. To this end, it is devastating the longest remaining stretch of undeveloped coastline on our Atlantic seaboard—bulldozing off the forest, leveling the dunes, draining the marshlands, and pumping landfill from the once-fertile fishing grounds offshore. The resulting lots are being peddled by a force of some six hundred high-pressure salesmen, working mostly in the northeastern states. Eventually they hope to entice into Palm Coast about 600,000 people, roughly equal to the population of New Orleans. ITT may well get away with it, in spite of considerable opposition from local residents and state agencies responsible for overseeing coastal development. As we all know, a corporation with billions at its disposal is hard to stop.

For all these reasons, it can be argued that building new towns is properly a task for public rather than private enterprise—or better yet, for the two working in partnership. Such a partnership offers the best chance, it seems to me, for the country to get by the end of the century anything like the 110 new towns and cities called for by the Committee on Urban Growth Policy.

Imagine what might happen if your state legislature authorized the setting up of a New Town Agency. It could solve with relative ease all the problems that are almost insuperable for the private developer.

It could assemble large tracts of land at a reasonable price by condemnation, under the ancient right of eminent domain. (Actually, as experience here and abroad has shown, this right would seldom have to be exercised. Its mere threat is enough to persuade most landowners to accept a fair offer.)

It could provide the necessary "patient money" in big amounts, by the sale of tax-exempt bonds or by the guarantee of private mortgages.

It would be able to resolve local political conflicts promptly through its authority to override when necessary zoning ordinances and building codes. (Again, this authority would rarely have to be invoked. But it is an invaluable stick to keep behind the door.)

It could locate its projects where they are most needed—

something the private developer often cannot do since he has to build where he can find land (and realize the greatest profit).

Its small permanent staff would do the basic planning and set standards for architecture, density, and open space —but usually would leave most of the building to private contractors.

It could attract industries more readily since it could offer, when necessary, subsidies and other inducements.

Again through subsidies, it could create a more natural mix of population, including low-income and elderly families. Private developers, of course, find it most profitable to build for the middle- and upper-income groups—although Columbia and some of the other new towns do have a few hundred federally subsidized homes for poorer people.

Most important of all, the Agency could reap the profits from the rising value of land in its new communities. These profits would be surer—and greater—than a private developer could hope for because the Agency could get its original land for less (through condemnation if necessary) and could avoid most of the other risks and delays of new town building. It could, in sum, harness old Henry George's principles for the public benefit. With prudent management, the resulting profits should more than cover both development costs and rental subsidies for the poor and elderly. The taxpayer, who now pays through the nose for every public housing project, would in effect be getting whole new cities for nothing.

This is not fantasy. Such an agency already is in operation: the New York State Urban Development Corporation. It is now building, among other things, three new towns, with more to come. It is by far the most innovative accomplishment of Nelson Rockefeller's long reign as governor. Because its example—and its mistakes—carry so many lessons for people in other states, it deserves a chapter to itself.

10.

An Idea Whose Time Has Not Quite Come

His enemies, who are plentiful, sometimes refer to the New York State Urban Development Corporation as Ed Logue's Fearsome Juggernaut. And on paper at least its powers are indeed fearsome. Moreover, the man who runs it has a reputation for ferocity. During World War II Edward J. Logue served as a bombardier in the Fifteenth Air Force, and his critics have suggested that his ideas for dealing with slums may have been born in that experience. With some reason. Before he became president of the Corporation, Logue had been largely responsible for rebuilding the central core of two cities, New Haven and Boston. In both cases he struck hard and fast, and for months their downtown areas looked much like London after the blitz.* Now they are often cited as the nation's most successful examples of urban renewal, but while Logue was making the dirt fly the complaints flew even faster. He was accused of insensitivity to the needs of real estate speculators, ward politicians, dis-

---

* Former Mayor Richard C. Lee told me that he took a group of visiting Russian officials on a tour of New Haven at the time when acres of the decayed business district had been torn down but new construction had not started.

"Please take us off your target list," he said to the Russians. "You can see that we have been demolished already."

Several of the visitors—who ostensibly understood no English—broke into laughter before the translator could relay Lee's quip.

placed slum dwellers, building trades unions, and contractors who were accustomed to sweetheart contracts with public agencies. Logue himself didn't realize how unpopular he had become until he ran for mayor of Boston; he took such a licking that he still winces when he talks about it.

In scores of other cities, of course, the men in charge of urban renewal have been far more sensitive to local needs and pressures—but in many of these places little of significance has happened. Even Logue's ill-wishers admit that when he is on the scene things do tend to happen. Consequently, when Governor Rockefeller named Logue in 1968 to manage the just-hatched Urban Development Corporation, with its unprecedented powers, many people—including the *New York Times* editorial writers and then-Mayor John Lindsay—expected the worst.

"Why, that man could tear down Manhattan," one New York politician told me at the time, "and nobody could lift a finger to stop him."

In theory, he could do just that. The Corporation was originally authorized by law to move into any community in the state, take whatever property it wanted by condemnation, raze any structures on the site, and replace them with homes, factories, schools, or office buildings, as it saw fit— all without paying any attention whatever to local zoning laws and building codes. It could have put up a vast Negro housing project in the middle of Scarsdale, the richest white suburb in the state. It could build whole new cities in the open countryside. Furthermore, it had a lot of money: to start with, $2 billion at its own command, possibly another $5 billion of private investment to be spent under its direction, and whatever federal loans and grants it could wangle out of Washington. (As he proved in New Haven and Boston, Logue is an expert wangler.) This unique array of armament was primarily Logue's idea. He had persuaded Governor Rockefeller that with less the new agency could not effectively attack the state's horrendous housing shortage.

But Logue never had any illusions that he could actually use to the full the authority which Rockefeller, and a reluctant legislature, had given him. The act setting up the Corporation had swept through the legislature on the wave of emotion following the assassination of Martin Luther King, Jr.—and even then it would not have passed if the governor had not turned on all the political pressure at his command. For three days you could hear the crackle of twisted elbows all over Albany. Consequently Logue realized that he did not have a genuine mandate from the legislators to attempt anything too radical. In the beginning, then, he used his unprecedented powers very gingerly indeed— though, as things turned out, not quite gingerly enough.

At our first meeting soon after the Corporation went into operation, I found it hard to understand Logue's reputation for ferocity. Instead of the hard-nosed, decision-snapping executive type I had expected, he turned out to be a rumpled, ruminative Irishman with a penchant (rare among public figures) for making wry jokes about himself. His office looked as if he had camped there overnight and hadn't yet decided whether to stay. A big relief map of New York State was mounted on the wall opposite his desk, but the floor was cluttered with cardboard boxes full of papers, and unhung pictures were stacked in a corner. He rummaged through a litter of documents on his desk until he found a paperback copy of *Parkinson's Law*.

"My bible," he said. "I keep it handy to remind me never to build up a big organization. If I did, I would become its prisoner. I mean to keep this outfit small and fast on its feet."

His strategy, he explained, was to limit the Corporation's

role to planning, policy-making, and stimulating action by others. Private contractors, architects, and investors were expected to build and operate virtually everything the Corporation would initiate. The Corporation's main job, as he originally saw it, would be to "put together packages"—that is, to line up the financing, acquire land, sketch out the broad outlines of a project, and enlist the participation of all the local, state, and federal agencies that might be concerned. Moreover, he promised to develop all his projects in close co-operation with local advisory committees—and, in the beginning, he indicated that the Corporation would not move into any community unless it was invited.

Clearly this was good politics. If the Corporation had started rampaging around like a bull elephant, as its early critics expected, it would quickly have become a political liability to Rockefeller; and if he had been defeated in the 1970 election, then his successor's first act probably would have been to shoot the elephant. In addition, it seemed to me to be good management. I had watched the failure of many hopeful governmental ventures, from New Deal days to President Johnson's War on Poverty, because their managers got bogged down in operations too grandiose for the bureaucracy to handle. So the sight of *Parkinson's Law* on Logue's desk struck me as reassuring.

Five years later, the Urban Development Corporation had accomplished considerably more than its critics—or even its friends—had expected. It had become, as Logue bragged in his 1972 report, "the most effective public or private organization in the country in providing housing for low- and moderate-income families." It had completed or had under construction more than 33,000 houses and apartments, plus twenty-seven civic, commercial, and industrial projects. More than half of its housing starts were in New York City, where the shortage was most desperate; the rest were scattered among fifty communities upstate. Unlike many federal housing projects, these were not prefabricated ghettos; they were built for a mix of ethnic, age, and income groups— roughly 70 per cent middle-income families, 20 per cent low-income, and 10 per cent for the elderly and hard-up. Architecturally, too, most of Logue's undertakings are superior to nearly all of the public housing I have seen elsewhere, including the new towns in Great Britain. The UDC projects do include a number of disappointments and missed opportunities; but probably fewer than one might expect, given the speed of its operations and the experimental nature of some of its undertakings.

To me, the most significant of Logue's ventures are the new communities—three of them under way by 1974. They alone have a chance of taking full advantage of the Henry George idea mentioned in the last chapter—that is, to siphon off the increase in property values, created by public investment, into the public purse instead of the speculator's.

The best known of these new communities is of course Welfare Island—the name likely to stick in popular usage although it has been officially redesignated as Roosevelt Island. Its spectacular site, in the middle of the East River just north of United Nations headquarters, was one of the few undeveloped large tracts within the boundaries of New York City. There UDC designed a community of five thousand homes, complete with schools, shops, a town center, a four-mile promenade for pedestrians and cyclists, and an aerial tramway to provide transportation to Manhattan pending the completion of a new subway line. The town will be virtually auto-free; electric mini-buses offer free transportation throughout the island, and an underground pneumatic system (almost noiseless) takes care of garbage disposal. Long before the new town was ready to welcome its first residents, Logue was sure that it would be a financial as well as a social success, although it will be some years before solid figures are available. To make it pay out, however, the project accommodates fewer low-income families than were originally proposed for it; and a number of architects have argued that the site planning did not make the best use of the uniquely scenic vistas available from almost every part of the island.

In population, the Roosevelt Island project is dwarfed by its less famous sisters: Lysander New Town, near Syracuse, and Audubon, on the northern outskirts of Buffalo. Lysander was designed to accommodate eventually about eighteen thousand people and to create new jobs in a labor-surplus area by means of an industrial park. The first plant it attracted was a Schlitz brewery—one of the world's largest—capable of producing more than five million barrels of malt beverages every year. This undertaking was blessedly free of hassles over its site because Logue was able to pick up 2,100 acres of vacant land, all in one piece, that had been used for an Army ordnance plant during World War II.

The third and largest of the new towns, on the other hand, was plagued by nearly three years of controversy and litigation between UDC and the local governments and school districts affected; they were afraid, naturally enough, that they would be overwhelmed by the thirty thousand new residents of Audubon. By the time construction finally got under way in 1973, most of the local people were apparently convinced that the project would be, at least, the lesser of the evils confronting them. For the new campus of the State University of New York, northeast of Buffalo, was expected to attract up to 140,000 residents into the area before the turn of the century. Unless advance plans were made to accommodate this growth in an orderly fashion, it could have been a disaster, blighting the entire northwestern corner of the state with sprawling suburbs. Consequently, Logue's men finally persuaded local officials to work with them on a master plan for the entire region, including extensive reconstruction of the Buffalo waterfront and downtown business district.

Audubon was designed as a key component in this plan. Adjoining the new campus, it will provide homes, shops, schools, churches, recreation areas, and generous amounts of open space for the newcomers. The initial investment, by UDC and private developers working under its aegis, will run to at least $500 million.

The increase in land values resulting from the Audubon development cannot be estimated even roughly at this writing. Neither does anyone know how much of it eventually will be recaptured through UDC to pay for the basic development costs—roads, sewers, and utilities—and to be returned as profit to the taxpayers. Potentially, however, both sums are very large indeed. Twenty years from now the Henry George dividend, so to speak, may be the most memorable—and instructive—feature of the undertaking.

Impressive as it is, the brief history of the Urban Development Corporation is by no means an unblemished success story. Indeed, at this stage it might be described as an idea whose time has not quite come.

For in 1973 when UDC was barely five years old, it suffered almost crippling attacks from two directions. One came from Washington when the Nixon administration cut off all funds—at least temporarily—for mortgage interest subsidies for low- and moderate-income housing. Nearly all of Logue's undertakings have depended partly on such federal subsidies, so when they were lost he had to cut back sharply on new projects. It seems likely that federal money eventually will start to flow again but probably in smaller amounts than UDC had been accustomed to. Even if the state increases its share of funding for lower-income housing (which is by no means certain), the Corporation will have to slow down its building at least temporarily to as little as one half of its initial pace.

Still more damaging was the state legislature's decision to strip away the Corporation's power to put up housing wherever it chose, regardless of local zoning and building codes. It took this action because Logue had finally decided—after much hesitation—to try to build a modest amount of low-income housing in wealthy Westchester County, just north of New York City. Specifically, he proposed to locate one hundred homes for low-income and elderly families in each of nine Westchester towns.

Logically his case was irrefutable. Westchester had long been woefully lacking in such housing, so that many of its teachers, clerical employees, and manual laborers had to commute from the city: an ironic reversal of the traditional traffic pattern. The need was growing fast as one big corporation after another moved its headquarters from Manhattan to the northern suburbs. A mere nine hundred homes could not possibly change the character of the county—which in any case was rapidly shifting from semi-rural to suburban to semi-urban. Moreover, by scattering the subsidized housing through nine communities, Logue hoped that the impact would be almost imperceptible.

Alas, the opposition to this modest undertaking was far from logical. On the contrary, Logue's Invasion—as it soon came to be known—set off the most passionate controversy that Westchester had known for generations. To many of the local residents, "low income" meant poverty, crime, drug addiction, and blacks. These were precisely the things that they had fled from New York City to escape, often at considerable cost and emotional strain. Now Logue was proposing, as they saw it, to bring the evils of the city into their snug suburban refuge. Worse yet, he was asking them, as taxpayers, to subsidize this unwanted influx. Never mind that nine hundred housing units was a relatively trivial amount. It might be the proverbial camel's nose under the tent; if Logue got away with this, he might try to build nine thousand next year—and in no time green and smiling Westchester could become another Harlem or, almost as dismaying, an extension of the Bronx.

The legislature listened to these irrational fears—expressed so uproariously in local hearings and protest meetings—and many an upstate representative suspected that his own constituents secretly harbored similar phobias. So the legislature voted to give any town or village authority to block a proposed UDC project by filing formal objections within thirty days after a public hearing. This limitation does not apply to cities, where Logue's powers—including his authority to set aside local zoning and building codes, and to ignore local sentiment if he dares—remain unchanged.

But the damage is severe and not to UDC alone. It means that the Corporation will have to concentrate its efforts, even more than in the past, in the big cities of the state. It ends the hope, however unrealistic it might have been, that UDC could help at least a few of the poor and black to escape from the ghettos; and it destroys any chance it may have had to bring a little better racial and economic balance to the rest of the state. From now on practically all that UDC can do in towns and villages is to build an occasional project for the elderly.

"Nobody minds having poor people for neighbors if they are old enough," Logue remarked with what I thought was a tinge of bitterness. "Nobody is scared of old folks, I guess."

Less calculable but probably more far-reaching harm was done beyond the borders of New York. Other states—California, for one—had been talking about setting up Development Corporations of their own since Logue had demonstrated that his invention is by far the most effective tool yet found for building publicly aided housing. After his debacle with the legislature, enthusiasm in other states became noticeably muted. Significantly, Governor Rockefeller did not veto the hamstringing legislation although he had vetoed a similar bill the previous year. Politicians throughout the country read his inaction to mean: "Rockefeller is getting ready to run for the Republican nomination for the presidency. He has to persuade the party pros in the boondocks that he really isn't as dangerous a radical as they have suspected. So he isn't going to stick his neck out on a public housing issue—and he probably is calculating sentiment correctly."

As a consequence of such reasoning, Development Corporations are not likely to blossom soon throughout the rest of the country. And when they do, they probably will lack the all-important authority to ignore restrictive zoning and building codes.

This means that our one best hope of building new towns on a large scale and in the right places is lost for the foreseeable future. It means, too, the loss of our best immediate chance to use Henry George's Money Machine in the public interest. Only public agencies, armed with powers like that of the original Urban Development Corporation, can assemble town sites at reasonable cost in the populous regions where they are most needed. Only such agencies can develop new towns in partnership with private capital and largely pay for them out of the profits from rising land values. Thus Logue's defeat was not only a sad day for New York State. It was a major setback everywhere for one of the most promising social inventions in sight. No doubt its time will come again; but for the needful present, the opportunity apparently is gone.

Some of Logue's associates now argue, privately, that the defeat was unnecessary. With hindsight, they suggest that

his timing was all wrong—that he should have known better
than to try to move into Westchester just after the 1972
elections had proved that conservative currents were running strong everywhere. It would have been wiser, in this
view, for UDC to have preserved its original powers, even if
it could not use them immediately.

Perhaps so. Logue has proved to be, on occasion, an
abrasive and belligerent fellow, in spite of my original impression to the contrary. If he had not forced the issue at an
ill-starred moment, a more conciliatory successor might
have been able to make good use of UDC's original powers at
a more auspicious time. On the other hand, Logue can argue
that the timid never find a good time to fight—and that
authority unused is likely to wither away, like an atrophied
muscle.

Many of Logue's critics oppose him on different grounds.
They contend that no official, nor any agency of the state,
should have the power to disrupt a community by bringing
in unwanted development, no matter how discreetly such
power might be used. To believers in the right of local communities to absolute home rule, this case sounds persuasive.
At times I am almost persuaded myself.

But on reflection, I feel that this argument overlooks two
points. Private developers can, and often do, disrupt communities by building ticky-tack speculative subdivisions, despite the opposition of earlier residents. And it is doubtful
whether such private invasions can be prevented by zoning
ordinances, however stringent, because such regulations
may violate another democratic right of long standing: the
right of a man to do what he likes with his own property.
Just how absolute this right may be has not yet been decided
definitely by the Supreme Court. Clearly a community can
stop a landowner from building a tannery in an established
residential district. But can it prevent him from building five
hundred homes, even though they will swamp the local

school system? The operations of an Urban Development Corporation, therefore, almost certainly will be less disruptive than the worst kind of speculative development, if only because it is more vulnerable to political pressure.

Moreover, no town or city really has the right to absolute home rule. Every local community is legally a creature of the state, and its authority can therefore be overridden by the state. At times the state's superior power can be tragically disruptive—as, for example, when a superhighway slices through an old community. Yet the state's need for the highway has generally been held superior to the town's wishes to fend it off.

In the long run, I believe, most states will use their superior authority to limit the exclusion of the poor and the black from affluent white suburbs. Exclusionary zoning already is under attack in many places. And the nation's sense of justice simply will not forever permit the inner cities to be strangled by a white suburban noose.

Eventually, then, the question will be: how to change the existing pattern with a minimum of disruption? Suburban block-busting by private speculators is not the best answer, as Yonkers and New Rochelle have learned. Consequently some kind of Urban Development Corporation—perhaps with its powers of invasion subject to a more elaborate process of hearings and review—may yet prove acceptable, if only as the lesser evil.

Moreover, the idea of a Development Corporation, with its unique ability to build self-financing new towns, is too good to be forgotten. One of these days it surely will be tried again, perhaps with better luck

11.

A Moderately Cheerful Note on a
Grim Subject—Property Taxes

Everybody hates the property tax, but nobody does anything about it. Well, hardly anybody.

A tax on real property is one of the oldest of Anglo-Saxon institutions. Its very name goes back to pre-feudal times when all land and buildings in theory belonged to the king: hence "real" meaning the royal tax. To this day it remains the chief source of money for local government, and the most unpopular.* Yet in spite of its unpopularity, it has persisted for three reasons. It yields a lot of revenue; next to the federal income tax, it skims more money off our bank accounts than any other kind of taxation. It is easy to collect. Nobody can hide a farm or building, and if you don't pay up promptly the king—or his successors, down to the lowliest county commissioner—can take your property away from you. And it is flexible. When a local government—city, county, school district, sewerage authority, or any of the other special agencies devised by the political imagination—needs more money, it is simple to add a few mills to the property tax. (Nobody ever saw a mill, of course, since it is a purely imaginary bit of money; tax collectors love to talk about it because it sounds so insignificant—only a one thou-

---

* As reported by the Advisory Commission on Intergovernmental Relations in its 1972 study, "Public Opinion and Taxes."

sandth part of a dollar, or a tenth of a cent. But it really isn't as innocuous as all that. The tax on my home in 1974, for example, was forty-nine mills for every dollar it was worth. Since the assessor valued it at $31,500, the bill came to $1,543.50.) If the town wants to cut taxes, on the other hand, it can shave a few mills off the rate—although hardly a man is still alive who can remember that happening. For in most localities, property taxes have risen inexorably, at least ever since World War II, as a result of inflation plus the growing cost of welfare and education, which eat up by far the largest share of the income from local taxes.

In contrast to its three advantages, the property tax has spectacular drawbacks:

1. *It is unfair.* The amount of taxable property in a community has no relationship to that community's needs. Consider two examples—by no means extreme—in Los Angeles County. The Beverly Hills school district had $50,885 worth of taxable property in 1969 for every pupil in its schools. But the Baldwin Park district, not very far away, had a tax base of only $3,706 for each of its pupils. Consequently Baldwin Park would have to levy taxes nearly fourteen times as high as Beverly Hills in order to raise the same amount of money for each student.* Personal income figures for the two communities are not available, but you can safely bet that a typical family in Beverly Hills is a lot richer than its Baldwin Park neighbors. In sum, those best able to pay get off lightly; while the poorer families either have to pay much heavier taxes or put up with a cheaper education for their children, or both. Similar cases are easy to find in every state. Not surprisingly, the loudest complaints about this kind of inequity come from elderly couples living on pensions or Social Security. Their modest incomes are fixed, but their

* From *Serrano* v. *Priest*, California Supreme Court, 1971.

school taxes keep going up—even though they no longer have any children in school. As a result many such families have had to give up the homes where they have spent most of their lives.

2. *It is a standing invitation to favoritism and corruption.* What a piece of real estate is worth is a matter of opinion—the assessor's opinion. Since he typically is a political appointee or an elected official with no special qualifications for estimating property values, it is easy for him to make honest mistakes. This is particularly true in localities where there have been no recent sales to give him a clue to current market prices. But he may well be suspected of worse than that. When similar houses in comparable neighborhoods are assessed at grossly different values, somebody is sure to wonder if he has been influenced—if not by a bribe, then by an old friendship, or by the temptation to retaliate against a member of a hostile political faction. Even when they are unfounded, such suspicions are a major reason for the unpopularity of the property tax.

3. *It encourages the worst kind of real estate development.* A builder is inevitably tempted to pass up vacant land in or near an existing community and to start a new subdivision on an outlying site where taxes are lower. The resulting suburban sprawl makes sound planning impossible and in the long run raises the cost of utilities, highways, water and sewerage, and other public services. It also leads to traffic congestion, wastage of scarce gasoline, and air pollution. The notorious smog of Los Angeles and Denver, to mention only two obvious cases, has its origin at least partly in the property tax.

4. *It forces public officials to act against the public interest.* This is its most damaging flaw and the least understood. Because local authorities naturally want to keep the tax rate as low as possible, they try to entice into their community those commercial enterprises that will yield a lot

of tax money—typically, manufacturing plants, motels, and shopping malls. This is known as "broadening the tax base." At the same time they are under heavy pressure to keep out of the community those people who will pay relatively little taxes but will demand a lot of expensive public services; that is, the poor, the black, and young families with several children of school age. This is known as "protecting the community."

In their efforts to attract industry, local officials must, of course, compete with every other community trying to do the same thing. They are tempted, therefore, to make concessions on zoning rules, building codes, and regulations for protecting the environment. The result all too often is an environmental mess—a lot more shopping malls, used-car lots, quick eateries, filling stations, rattlesnake farms, and marginal factories than the community really needs (except for the taxes they pay), and these "civic improvements" are likely to be jerry-built eyesores, located in the wrong places. You can see this happening in the strip developments that border every suburban highway. The most nightmarish example I know of is U.S. 1 as it crosses New Jersey—though you could argue that the Florida section of the same route is almost as bad. Our conventional wisdom blames commercial greed for such environmental disasters; but it seldom notes that an underlying cause is the property tax, which encourages this particular form of anti-social greediness.

To "protect the community," on the other hand, suburban officials are tempted to resort to fiscal zoning. That is, they may require that new homes be built only on large lots— sometimes two to four acres—so expensive that young families and the poor can't afford them. Often, too, they forbid apartment houses and impose building codes that raise building costs unnecessarily. Such devices are remarkably effective in walling out "undesirables," who might overload the school and welfare systems. They are partly responsible, therefore, both for the nation's housing shortage and for the segregation of the suburbs from the inner-city ghettos. Here again, the villain is not simply stupidity or ill will; the very nature of the property tax compels officeholders—and their constituents—to behave in anti-social ways.

The competition between communities—for more big tax-payers and fewer poor people and schoolchildren—also inhibits local officials who understand how bad the property tax is and would like to shift to a better alternative. Either a local income tax or a sales tax, for example, might be a good idea, at least as a supplement to the property tax. But any town that imposes such taxes would, presumably, find it harder to attract industry, and some of its present big tax-payers might well move to a neighboring community that doesn't have them. Any solution to the property tax problem, therefore, has to be sought beyond the community. No local taxing authority can solve it alone.

By the early seventies, the search for wider solutions had become fairly lively. It was stimulated both by growing public discontent with the property tax and by a series of court decisions holding that it violates the equal-protection clause of the Fourteenth Amendment. As the California Supreme Court ruled in the case of *Serrano* v. *Priest,* it makes "the quality of a child's education a function of the wealth of his parents and neighbors." At this writing, the supreme courts of seven other states—Minnesota, Texas, Wyoming, Arizona, Kansas, Michigan, and New Jersey—have made similar findings, though the United States Supreme Court has not yet ruled on the issue. Whatever the latter decides, it seems likely that the pressure will grow for the states to find some better way to pay for their schools.

One solution would be for the states to take over full responsibility, with some help from Washington. Hawaii, in fact, has done just that. Most other states have been moving rather gingerly in the same direction; in 1930 local school districts raised nearly 83 per cent of the money needed to build and run their schools, but by 1970 they were raising only a little more than half. The rest came from the states—40.7 per cent—and the federal government—6.6 per cent.

If all states followed the Hawaiian example, local property taxes could be sharply reduced, since education costs would be paid mostly by income and sales taxes and other state revenues. Every student would then get the same amount of money for his schooling as every other student within his state. Considerable inequalities would remain from one state to another; but they could be leveled out, in theory, by federal contributions.

Such an arrangement looks attractive, not only because it would mitigate the evils of the property tax, but because for the first time every youngster in the country would get an even break in the cost of his education. But for the foreseeable future, it is probably impossible politically. For in education, as in everything else, he who pays the piper eventually calls the tune; and most communities are not willing to let control of their schools drift into the hands of state authorities. For the present, at least, they would prefer to put up with the traditional system, bad as it is.

But perhaps not forever. I have a hunch, with no hard evidence to back it up, that an increasing share of school costs gradually will be shifted from local communities to the states, as they have been shifting ever since 1930. I also think it likely that the federal contribution to education will grow—and that Washington eventually will take over virtually the entire burden of welfare. That seems, at least, to be the trend of the many recent proposals for revenue sharing and welfare reform.

I am not sure this would be altogether a good thing. It would get rid of the property tax except for small levies to pay the salaries of local officials. It would end at last the

grosser inequalities in education. It would wipe out some of
the incentives for poor people to migrate from the countryside to the big cities and from the backward states to those
with higher welfare payments and better schools. These
would be no small improvements. I am not sure that they
would offset the probable loss of local control over education—which I, like my neighbors, value highly. Maybe some
social inventor will come up with a scheme for shifting the
cost of schools to the state and federal level while leaving
policy securely in local hands; but so far as I can find, no
such idea has yet emerged.

Meanwhile, however, an idea has emerged that may get
rid of some of the worst effects of the property tax. It originated, like so many other bright ideas for civic improvement, in Minnesota. Like the Twin Cities Metropolitan
Council, it sprang from a study of a Citizens League committee. This one was headed by Earl F. Colborn, Jr., and its
report was published in 1969 under the rather grandiose
title: "Breaking the Tyranny of the Local Property Tax."
The basic strategy it outlined was first suggested by Charles
R. Weaver, a member of the Minnesota House of Representatives, and F. Warren Preeshl, a suburban school board
member; although I suspect that the invaluable Ted Kolderie, director of the League, may also have had something
to do with it.

The objective was simple: to halt the destructive competition among all the towns and cities in the metropolitan area
for new industries. The means was ingenious: to spread at
least part of the tax money gained from a new industry—or
motel, or shopping mall—throughout the three thousand
square miles of the metropolitan area rather than leaving all
of it to the lucky community where the newcomer happened
to alight.

To carry this out, the Minnesota legislature passed a law

in 1971 that, in effect, pools 40 per cent of the assessed
valuation of all new commercial and industrial developments within the metropolitan area. Suppose, for example,
that a new factory goes up in the suburban community of
Edendale; its assessed value is $5 million. Instead of keeping
all the yield from the property tax on this plant, Edendale
would get only 60 per cent, or $3 million, as the increase in
its tax base. The remaining 40 per cent would be pooled
along with a similar share of all other new commercial and
industrial growth within the boundaries of the Twin Cities
Metropolitan Council. The total pool would then be redis-
tributed among all the three-hundred-odd taxing districts in
the area, roughly on a basis of population.

This may sound complicated, but in fact it is not. It is
merely a fairly simple device for pooling not tax revenues,
but a part of the growth in the tax base. Each community
keeps control over its own tax rate and decides as always
how its tax revenues shall be spent. But since a good part of
the benefit from new growth is spread out among all the
residents of the metropolitan area, any particular community has less incentive to compete in harmful ways for
commercial investment. Some incentive persists, of course,
since Edendale keeps more of the benefit from growth than
it contributes to the pool; but presumably the temptation of
cutthroat competition is reduced by at least 40 per cent. And
if the legislature should decide in the future to increase the
pooled share gradually to something approaching 100 per
cent, such temptation would disappear entirely. Most pro-
ponents of the scheme hope this will happen—and that the
area affected by the pooling will be expanded to cover not
just the metropolis but the whole state.

How well the idea will work in practice was still unknown
at this writing, in 1974, because the constitutionality of the
new law was being challenged in the courts. (One small
community, the village of Burnsville, brought the suit be-

cause it felt that it might lose more than it would gain from the plan.) But even before it went into effect, the Twin Cities base-sharing system was attracting keen interest from other states; the indications were that it, or something closely akin, would soon be tried elsewhere.

Different ideas for reforming the property tax to get rid of at least some of its bad effects are cropping up in a fair number of other places. Boston is taxing new buildings only half as heavily as old ones in hopes of reviving its long-stagnant construction industry. Southfield, Michigan, took a lesson from old Henry George's primer and sharply increased the tax on land while at the same time cutting the tax on improvements. Some acreage which was assessed at only $2,400 in 1961 is now assessed at $100,000. The effect was to penalize speculators, slum lords, and other land-owners—of parking lots, for instance, or two-story "taxpayer buildings"—who were not making the best and most intensive use of their property. The result was a notable boom in office building construction.

Vermont has been afflicted by soaring land prices as a result of the explosive development of its relatively un-spoiled landscape for vacation homes, ski lodges, and lake resorts. The average value of a Vermont acre more than doubled in five years. As a consequence, many poor and elderly Vermonters faced a doubling of their property taxes although their incomes remained unchanged. Their only recourse, then, was to sell out to wealthy developers— "furrin land-grabbers," as they came to be called, since most of them came from other states. The local resentment built up so rapidly that in 1973 the legislature made two unprece-dented changes in the tax laws. One of them imposes heavy capital gains taxes—up to 60 per cent—on speculators who reap a big profit out of quick deals in land: the larger the profit and the shorter time the land is held, the heavier the tax. The other innovation links property taxes to income; a family earning less than $4,000 a year will never have to pay more than 4 per cent of that amount in property tax, and even those making more than $16,000 will be assured of a tax ceiling of 6 per cent. Since so many native Vermonters are elderly couples living on small farms and meager incomes, this law protects about a third of the state's households from forced eviction no matter how high land prices may climb.

It is still too early to tell how these experiments, and Minnesota's, will work out in the long run. But each of them is one more indication that the venerable property tax is being re-examined—that more and more people are coming to realize that it may well be, in the words of a National League of Cities study:

"The very worst of all taxes . . . a weird combination of overtaxation and undertaxation, an incentive tax for what we don't want, and a disincentive tax for what we do want. It harnesses the profit motive backward instead of forward to both urban renewal and urban development. Too often, it makes it more profitable to misuse and underuse land than to use it wisely and fully, more profitable to let buildings decay than to improve or replace them."

And each innovation of the kind mentioned here is a reminder that we don't really have to put up with this nonsense just because it has been with us longer than the Doomsday Book.

12.

Appalachia and Its First Proconsul

Ever since Daniel Boone shot bears there, Appalachia has been an economic basket case. It is an oblong patch of mountains and misery, stretching from a corner of Mississippi on the south to a corner of New York at its northern end. Its chief distinction is the densest concentration of poverty in America, and after World War II, it seemed to be going from bad to worse. Its only significant products were coal, timber, and children. All three had been pouring out of the hills for a long time, leaving the countryside steadily more impoverished—its slopes ravaged by strip miners and slash-and-run lumbermen, its streams polluted, its towns drained of brainpower and leadership. The loss of people hurt most: two and a half million of them in a single decade following the war. When they got to Chicago or Cleveland or Detroit they were derided as hillbillies, but they were the best Appalachia had: those with enough initiative, energy, and education to get out and try to make a new start somewhere else.

On May 8, 1960, Millard Tawes, then governor of Maryland, asked some of the other Appalachia governors to meet him in Annapolis to see whether they could figure out some way to stop this hemorrhage. It might help, he thought, if they pooled their ideas and resources (though they didn't have much of either)—and together they might stand a better chance of prying a really big satchel of money out of the federal treasury.

The moment seemed right. President John F. Kennedy had, with shocked surprise, seen massive poverty for the first time while he was campaigning there; and he had a special soft spot for West Virginia since his primary victory in that state had been a turning point in his drive for the presidency. When the Appalachian governors called on him, he agreed that something drastic should be done to help the region, although neither he nor they knew exactly what.

So he set up the inevitable study group, which labored mightily and brought forth a Plan. By that time Lyndon Johnson was in the White House. He sold the idea to Congress as part of the martyred President's legacy and finally —five years after Tawes's first meeting—the Appalachian Regional Commission was born.

Its orders were simple: to make Appalachia prosper and put its people to work. But nothing else about it was simple or even familiar. It was to be financed mostly with federal money—nearly half a billion dollars in the first three years —but it is *not* a federal agency. It is a hybrid bastard, part federal, part state, part something that neither of its parents could recognize. It has two heads. Known as co-chairmen, one of them is a governor—initially Mills Godwin of Virginia—who speaks for the states; the other is a presidential appointee who speaks for Washington. Together with the twelve other Appalachian governors, they make up a sort of corporate board of directors. In addition the governors have a full-time henchman to look after their interests from day to day. He and the federal co-chairman sit in neighboring offices at the Commission's headquarters, a nondescript Plate Glass Modern building at 1666 Connecticut Avenue in Washington. You might call them, I guess, co-equal board chairmen. Each carries a veto, so the Commission can do nothing significant unless they are in agreement. In another neighboring office sits (when he isn't pacing the floor) the executive director of the Commission—the one person who, more than anybody else, is responsible for its success or failure. During the formative years, that job was held by a remarkable man named Ralph R. Widner.

Any management expert could tell you that such a surrealist organization chart would never work, if only for the biblical rule that no man can serve two masters. In practice, it has worked reasonably well although there has been plenty of tugging back and forth: if you are optimistic, you can call that "creative tension." The reason that the machinery hasn't frozen up is that the President's man—there have been several of them—and the governors' man—from the beginning until this writing, John D. Whisman—think alike on most matters and pull comfortably in harness (well, most of the time) with the executive director. Then too, their assignment is an exciting one, which always tends to minimize bureaucratic infighting.

That assignment might have daunted Hercules, not to say the three bureaucrats mainly responsible for carrying it out. Their domain includes 19 million people in thirteen states.* Its boundaries are not very sensibly drawn. They encompass only one whole state—West Virginia. In theory, they include the poorer, more mountainous parts of the other states, but in some cases these inclusions are hard to justify by either geographical or economic reasoning. The southern tier of counties in New York, for example, is really not all that poor, but it was thrown into the region to ensure the support of Bobby Kennedy, then senator from the state. The Commission's flow of money has been modest in comparison

---

* Alabama, Georgia, Kentucky, Maryland, Mississippi, New York, North Carolina, Ohio, Pennsylvania, South Carolina, Tennessee, Virginia, and West Virginia.

with the needs. Its authority is narrowly limited. The region's inhabitants, moreover, are probably the least governable on this continent: belligerently individualistic, most of them, suspicious, badly educated, apathetic, underfed, conservative to the marrow, and often somewhat alcoholic.

Given all this, where to start? For guidance the Commission had a report prepared during the preliminary study stage by a consultant, Litton Industries, supposedly expert on the location of manufacturing plants. It suggested a basic strategy. Don't dribble the money away in little handouts to every needy community. Instead, concentrate investment in a few "growth areas," which had at least a possibility of developing into major industrial centers. Litton named forty-four such places in order of potential.

While this may have made sense economically, politically it was a born loser. For the list contained no communities in West Virginia and eastern Kentucky, where poverty was most acute, and in all states the proposed growth centers were too few. If the agency had announced that most of its states had only four or five towns with any real prospects for the future and that all their other communities should be written off as hopeless and therefore undeserving of federal money, the resulting political tornado would have wiped it out overnight. Fortunately Widner, the executive director, and John L. Sweeney, the first federal co-chairman, had enough political sensitivity to understand this very well indeed. They liked the idea of concentrating investment where it would be most effective, but they weren't about to say where these places were. That uncomfortable task could be left to the individual states, with a little general guidance from the Commission.

Its chief guideline was a request that every state should submit a development plan to be updated year by year. This plan should identify potential growth centers and suggest in order of priority the public investments that ought to be made to help them grow. For the first time in our history, states were required to undertake some coherent economic planning; and they were told (very politely) that if the Commission did not like their plans, the dollar spigot would remain firmly closed. This ukase went out from Widner's office in the summer of 1966. At the time, I never thought he could get away with it.

He did, because Widner is a superb tactician. He is expert, among other things, in keeping a low silhouette and moving gently, gently through the underbrush of government. He knows well how to let other people—governors, for example—take the credit; and, incidentally, to take the heat for unpopular decisions, such as the designation of growth centers. Before announcing a startling initiative, such as the demand for state planning, he consulted endlessly and with apparently infinite tact all of the people concerned. When he made his move, therefore, he had the approval, or at least the acquiescence, not only of his co-chairmen but of the White House, the key men on Capitol Hill, and all thirteen of the governors.

In other ways, too, Widner was an untypical bureaucrat. He had none of the cautious pomposity that so often characterizes the high-level civil servant. A onetime desk man for the *New York Times*, he brought with him the newspaperman's working habits—relaxed, outgoing, a little cluttered, on first-name terms with his staff. His casual, almost breezy, manner concealed a solid academic grounding in government (Duke and New York universities, a congressional fellowship from the American Political Science Association) plus eight years of experience in both state and federal jobs. Because he had no ambition to run for any elective office, politicians did not view him as a potential rival and so came more easily to trust him. To these assets you might add the energy of youth. Widner was only thirty-five when he became America's first proconsul.

A former White House aide who talked to me about Widner said, "For God's sake, don't call him a proconsul. That word will scare Congress to death."

But I can't think of any other word that comes even close to suggesting the nature of his job. Like the old Roman proconsuls, he directed the operations of the central government within a specific territory. Besides, I don't think congressional nervousness is justified. So far, the Appalachian Regional Commission has not usurped any of the powers of the elected state and local officials, nor of Congressmen. On the contrary, it has markedly increased the effectiveness of at least some of the Appalachian state, city, and county governments, so that they can now embark on undertakings that previously would have had to be done (if at all) by old-line Washington bureaucrats.

The first reaction to Widner's request for development plans was one of consternation. Except for New York, under the stern rule of Nelson Rockefeller, none of them had any real capability to make a plan. Some governors regarded the whole idea as an affront, another instance of Washington's whimsical appetite for red tape; what they really wanted was for the Commission to hand over their share of its money and then go away. Others saw it as an opportunity. In the end, all of them went along because Sweeney and Widner persuaded them that without some defensible economic planning, the region could not get continuing appropriations from Congress.

One of the governors who grasped the planning idea as an opportunity was Robert E. McNair of South Carolina, hitherto notorious for its conservatism and Confederate nostalgia. Only six of the state's counties fall within the Appa-

lachian region, so he might have tinkered up a plan for
them alone. Instead he decided to plan for the whole state,
following the Commission's guidelines and principles
throughout. Since the state had no planning staff to speak
of, McNair hired an impeccably conservative Wall Street
consulting firm, Moody Investors Service, to do the job for
him.

Its recommendations shook the juleps right out of the
palsied hands of the state's old ruling elite. In effect, Moody
told them, you can no longer hope to coax worthwhile industries into South Carolina with the traditional bait—tax ex-
emptions, subsidies, the promise of docile nonunion labor.
At best these lures would attract only declining, low-wage
companies—a shirt manufacturer, maybe, or a carpet
weaver who couldn't make it up north. To hook modern,
expanding industries in chemicals or electronics or instrument making, you have to offer something quite different.
What they want, first of all, is an intelligent, educated, and
healthy labor force. Before it could offer that, South Carolina would have to build a network of vocational schools and
make dramatic improvements in health care—including the
training of a corps of young paramedical professionals.

The first beneficiaries of these measures, obviously, would
be the blacks and the poor whites—neither of whom had
ever stood high on the state's agenda. By a near-miracle of
persuasion, McNair got the legislature not only to see the
wisdom of the plan, but to vote new taxes to help finance it.
To put it into effect, he decided—at the Commission's urg-
ing—to depend not on the counties but on local development
districts of the kind described in Chapters 3 and 4. All six of
the Appalachian counties fall within the district known as
the South Carolina Appalachian Council of Governments,
managed by Donald R. Hinson, whom we met earlier. Because his district alone is authorized to call on the Commission for money and technical help—and because Hinson is

such an able fellow—his district is more successful than most. But the whole state is now healthier and more hopeful than it has been at any time since the Civil War; and for that the development plan deserves a good share of the credit.

To my sorrow, I can't say as much for all the Appalachian states. As I went through their plans in Washington and traveled through most of the states to see what was actually happening, I discovered that the planning efforts are lamentably spotty. Only in a few cases—South Carolina, Georgia, Pennsylvania, New York, and one or two others—can the plans be described as both professional and effective. In each of these states, the planning offices are well staffed; they are in close, often daily, touch with the governor; and they get a good input of information and project proposals from the development districts. Most importantly, they handle planning as a continuing process, tightly linked to the governor's budget and legislative program. They have grown far beyond the old-fashioned notion that a plan is a one-time blueprint for Utopia, with nobody in particular responsible for carrying it out.

Of most of the remaining states, it can be said that they are making weak but hopeful efforts. Characteristically, they have a small and not very expert planning staff or depend heavily on outside consultants, and they are working on the fringes of government rather than at the center. Generally the governors concerned are aware of these weaknesses and are trying, with various degrees of vigor, to mend them.

A few states have to go at the bottom of the list: West Virginia (which at this writing has not even organized development districts), Ohio, and Mississippi. Their planning can only be described as rudimentary—probably because neither the voters nor the main power groups are convinced of its value; naturally, then, the governors and legislatures pay it little attention.

The Commission's Washington staff, which is responsible for reviewing the states' plans, has never been happy with most of them. It has done what it could to beef up the planning process—offering technical assistance, criticizing poorly justified programs, suggesting new projects, and since 1973 offering management grants to improve planning staffs. Whether it might have been more demanding is a matter of political judgment. Probably not much, given the role of the states on the Commission itself; obviously it is hard, and dangerous, to crack down on your own boss. Moreover, loud demands for better planning were not likely to accomplish much. After all, the idea is a relatively new one; expert planners are scarce; and few states anywhere in the country provide the strong, well-structured government that good planning implies. Gradually this will change—I hope, and I guess I believe—as state governments are reorganized to do a better job: a process now under way in a good many states and in a variety of ways, ranging from the writing of new constitutions to the providing of better pay and staff assistance for legislators.

A personal digression. As we have noted, the federal demand for better planning—coming from the Office of Management and Budget and several other agencies as well as the Appalachian Regional Commission—has forced many states, cities, and development districts to turn to outside consultants, at least until they can build up planning staffs of their own. As a consequence, a small but highly influential profession has sprung into being: the free-lance planning consultants. One of the most successful of these firms is Hammer, Siler, George Associates, with offices in Washington and Atlanta. It is the creation of that same Philip Hammer mentioned in Chapter 3, who in an earlier stage of his career helped to invent and get established the first local development districts. Naturally enough, in the beginning the firm worked largely for such districts in the South where Hammer was best known. More recently it has acquired a much wider clientele throughout this country and abroad. One of its latest assignments came from the Appalachian Regional Commission itself, which wanted an outside appraisal of its work—a study that, alas, is still under way at this writing; it would have been an invaluable source of material for this chapter.

Hammer is now regarded as one of the leaders of the profession and has served as president of the American Society of Planning Officials. His career has given me much personal satisfaction, since his first experience in government was working for me in the Farm Security Administration of the New Deal era. Today if I were a young man and just out of college, as he was then, I think I would apply for a job in his firm or a similar one, because I can't imagine a more useful and interesting line of work.

In spite of the immature quality of much of the state planning, it is producing a fair amount of progress toward one of the Commission's original goals. That is the building up of medium-sized cities: the whole purpose of its concentration of investment in growth centers.

As Ralph Widner once remarked to me, "America has two choices in its future: (a) urbanization or (b) urbanization."

What he meant was that we can continue to let a good part of our population drift into the great agglomerate metropolises, such as New York and Los Angeles, or we can deliberately plan inducements to channel a bigger share of our growing population into medium-sized cities, more manageable and more livable. The latter is the policy that I believe the country is gradually, almost unconsciously, adopting, for the reasons mentioned in Chapter 2. Certainly it is

the policy the Appalachian Regional Commission has followed from the beginning.

Appalachia has always been short of cities. Most of its
people live in crumbling small towns or on starvation farms
at the head of some God-forgotten hollow. Its only metropolitan areas are Pittsburgh and Birmingham, both dominated by the elderly and sluggish steel industry. Unfortu-
nately a number of fast-growing cities lie just outside its
borders: along the coast and the Piedmont to the east,
booming Atlanta and the Gulf ports to the south, in the
Mississippi Valley to the west.

Appalachia also has lived in isolation. Only one modern
highway crosses it from east to west. Because of the difficult
terrain and the states' chronic lack of money, the region
never had even a good network of secondary roads, and its
railways and airports were equally inadequate. Lacking
transport, its towns had no chance to attract much industry.

So one of the Commission's first moves was to plan a web
of modern highways in the belief that they would do more
than any other one thing to revive the region's economy.
Growth centers would begin to burgeon along these routes
presumably, and especially at their nodes. Besides, highway
construction would inject a lot of quick money into the
region's economic bloodstream; and it would produce early,
visible results—which the Commission needed to survive
politically. Consequently road-building has always been
much the largest item in the Commission's budget; about
half of its planned 2,600 miles of highways were either
completed or under construction by 1974.

The Commission has never drafted a detailed, overall
economic plan for the region. Its only region-wide planning
has been for transport—highways and airports—together
with a related program for developing recreation areas and
tourism. Its reasoning was that the transport network would
provide a structural frame that would determine almost

automatically the location of growth centers and the flow of investment. Within that frame, the detailed planning could be left to the states.

And so it has worked out, in a rough sort of way. At this writing the states have designated about eighty growth centers; the number grows from time to time in response to local political pressures. They include about 80 per cent of the region's population. Under a more rigorous, less political, definition of growth centers, such as Litton originally proposed, the number would be smaller and less inclusive. Yet the concentration of the Commission's investments has been tighter than these figures would suggest. More than half of its funds have gone into only 15 per cent of the 397 counties in Appalachia. Generally these have been counties organized into fairly efficient development districts, such as those described earlier under the management of Messrs. Dayton and Hinson. Generally again, the growth centers really are growing; my subjective judgment is that in most of them now a man not only can make a decent living, but live a good life.

On the other hand, sixty-five counties have received no Commission money at all. These and some others will remain pockets of poverty, at least till the present generation dies off or moves away. I have seen counties in eastern Kentucky where it will never be possible to build a factory or even a good-sized school because there literally is not enough level land. Nevertheless, many of the people who live there would rather starve than move away. They are devoted to the steep laurel-and-pine-covered slopes where they and their ancestors since Colonial days have eked out an existence by hunting, raising a few hogs and vegetables, and a little moonshining.

In addition to highways, the Commission has financed hundreds of other projects, some suggested by its own staff, others originating with the states and their development districts. Vocational education schools have been the most numerous—more than six hundred of them, costing nearly a quarter of a billion dollars. Other popular undertakings have been the reclamation of land ruined by strip mining, control of water pollution, health facilities of many kinds from ambulances to hospitals, libraries, housing, and industrial parks. The money is parceled out among the states according to a series of formulae, adopted in the early days of the Commission. These take into account population, per capita income, the percentage of young people not in school (for vocational education grants), the number of low-income farms (for land conservation programs), the number of mines (for mine restoration), and several similar factors. Surprisingly, the states have all accepted this method of splitting up the pie as fair enough, so there has been almost none of the squabbling one might have expected. Credit for this contribution to interstate amity belongs to Monroe Newman, the staff economist who originally worked out the formulae.

Besides its own money, the Commission had channeled into Appalachia about half a billion dollars by 1972 from other government agencies. Widner believed that one of the most useful jobs for himself and his small staff was to serve as Washington lobbyists for his thirteen states, making sure that they would get every dollar available from the Department of Agriculture, Housing and Urban Development, the Office of Economic Opportunity, and countless other federal paymasters. He endeavored, too, to see that such funds were spent in accordance with the state development plans—although in this he was only partially successful. Since the Commission had no authority to give orders to other government agencies, persuasion was his only weapon. Amid the rivalries of Washington, that often was not enough. For example, the anti-poverty warriors of the Economic Development Administration in the Department of Commerce openly challenged the Commission's growth center strategy. In giving out their money, they preferred a policy of "worst first"—that is, to dole out their grants to the neediest communities, regardless of the prospects for economic development.

How successful is the Appalachian Regional Commission?

The question is hard to answer with figures alone, because the venture is a relatively young one. Many of its investments, such as the highway network, are incomplete; others, such as the vocational schools, have just begun to pay off; results from others, such as the health and child development programs, cannot be truly measured for at least a generation.

It can be said that by 1973 the Commission had brought about the investment of more than $4 billion from state and federal funds and had induced private investments in the region of many, but not precisely calculated, millions more. Spending from its own appropriations was still running at the rate of nearly $300 million a year, a sum more than matched by contributions from state and other federal sources. Measured against a space program or the military budget, these sums may sound trivial—but in a region starved for capital throughout two centuries, the impact has been considerable. For example, the total of personal incomes in Appalachia rose by more than $14 billion, or 36 per cent, between 1965 and 1969. The number of its people living below the poverty line dropped from 31 per cent to 18 per cent in the decade ending in 1970. During the same decade, net migration out of the new region came to a virtual halt. Within the five years before 1970, 545,000 new jobs were created in Appalachia; but because of the growth of population, unemployment remained a fraction of a per cent higher than the national level. Even so, this was a notable gain over those decades when Appalachia chronically had the worst unemployment problem in the nation.

On the other hand, per capita income is still only 80 per cent of the national average, so the region has a long way yet to go. And it is of course impossible to specify how much of Appalachia's progress should be credited to the Commission, or whether the gains might have been as big (or bigger) if equal sums of money had been injected through regular federal agencies.

In popular and political terms, however, there is no question about the Commission's success. In 1971 the Nixon administration tried to abolish the Appalachian Regional Commission along with a number of other anti-poverty and social-action programs left over from the Kennedy-Johnson era. Congress voted overwhelmingly to keep the Commission going—in the Senate by the remarkably lopsided and non-partisan vote of 77 to 3. All thirteen of the region's governors have given the experiment their steady support—and on one memorable day enthusiastic statements about it were issued by Senator John Stennis of Mississippi and the National Association for the Advancement of Colored People. So far as I know, that was the first day they ever agreed on anything.

Perhaps the best measure of the Appalachian Regional Commission's value is the recurring demand that it be duplicated in other parts of the country, as we shall see in the next chapter.

Ralph Widner resigned from the Commission late in 1971 to head up a new foundation, the Academy for Contemporary Problems, in Columbus, Ohio. He was worn by six years of grinding, often contentious, labor. He felt, I believe, that he had made about all the original contributions he could. He had laid the groundwork for the agency, recruited its capable and nonpolitical staff, developed its novel strategies, and built lasting support for it in Congress and throughout the region. Besides, he saw little chance for further innovation under the Nixon administration.

His leaving was unpublicized, and he himself remained virtually unknown except among the circle of people he had worked with. His self-effacement was, of course, a professional asset; but it also seemed to me a pity because his career in government was one of the most brilliant I have observed in my time. If it were more widely known, the example might have attracted many able young people into government service. I trust that he found it satisfying. After all, he was the principal founding father of a new kind of institution, which is changing the lives of millions of people and which seems fairly certain to be imitated, eventually, in other places.

A note for people who would like to know more about the Appalachian Regional Commission and its detailed workings.

The best sources of information are the Commission's annual reports and its internal working papers. The reports are available from the office of the current executive director, Harry Teter, Jr., 1666 Connecticut Avenue, Washington, D.C. 20235. The working papers are harder to come by, but the Commission staff and the state planning offices have been remarkably free in showing their research studies, directives, and evaluations to any serious inquirer.

So far little has been published about the Commission, aside from a few magazine and newspaper articles. A good account of its origins is included in *Politics and Policy: The Eisenhower, Kennedy, and Johnson Years*, by James L. Sundquist (Brookings Institution, 1968). *The Political Economy of Appalachia: A Case Study in Regional Integration*, by Monroe Newman (Lexington Books, 1972) is the most comprehensive book on the subject. A well-considered evaluation of the Commission (though, in my view, a slightly pessimistic one) is contained in *Between State and Nation,* by Martha Derthick (Brookings Institution, 1974).

By far the best way to get a feel for the Commission's work is to visit the field offices of a few of the local development districts. Almost any one of them contains a lode of material for feature articles, academic papers, and scholarly books yet unwritten.

13.

Ten Provinces, Maybe?

When Ned Breathitt was governor of Kentucky, back in the mid-sixties, he worked out a sound and imaginative plan to rejuvenate his state, which could do with a lot of rejuvenation. He was encouraged, he told me, both by John F. Kennedy's brave speeches about New Frontiers and by Lyndon B. Johnson's declaration of the War on Poverty. After listening to them, naturally, he counted on a good deal of help from Washington.

For the new homes Kentucky so badly needed, Breathitt hoped to get financing from the Department of Housing and Urban Development. Then he would go to the Department of Health, Education, and Welfare for the schools to go with the new homes and for some improvements in the state's system—if you could call it that—of medical care. And somewhere else to get money for sewers and water supply; at least five different agencies, he found, were authorized to help build such facilities, so he had to shop around to see where he could get the best deal. From the Labor Department and the Office of Economic Opportunity he thought he might get some job training for the unskilled poor people he had in abundance. And the Agriculture Department claimed to be ready to help in lots of ways, if he cared to ask for its money and expert advice.

His undertaking turned out to be more strenuous and travel-fraught than Breathitt had anticipated. Nearly all these federal agencies had field offices that were supposed to help state and local officials in making out applications and meeting requirements. But none of these, as it happened, were in Kentucky. To talk to HUD, the governor had to go to Atlanta. The HEW regional office was in Raleigh, North Carolina. The Labor Department people he had to see nested in Chicago, the Small Business Administration office was in Philadelphia, and OEO's "field office" for his region was, quaintly, in Washington.

Ned's obvious strategy was to get all these regional representatives together in one room somewhere, so he could explain his plans, reach some common understanding on what was feasible, and get a commitment from each agency on how its piece of money could be fitted into the jigsaw puzzle. But this proved impossible. Such busy men couldn't spare time from their paperwork. Besides, they were not accustomed to gathering, at the behest of a mere governor, to see whether they could work together—which they weren't accustomed to either.

Before he left office, Ned Breathitt did accomplish a good deal for the social and economic health of his state—but nowhere near as much as he had once hoped. And he had concluded that "the mess in Washington" was an understatement; the federal government was all messed up in the field too.

His experience was typical of the trauma state and local officials had been suffering ever since federal programs began to proliferate back in the thirties. It got worse when the Johnson administration began to spawn new programs to cure a wide variety of social ills. Nobody knows how many there were, but the tally certainly went above a thousand. All of them were well intentioned. They were meant to feed hungry people, clear slums, upgrade police departments, beautify highways, and any number of other nice things. Washington was eager to ladle out money—$27 billion in fiscal 1970, for example—to the towns and states that it expected to carry out these undertakings.

But the Johnson vision did not, to put it gently, work out exactly as intended. For each of the programs was enacted piecemeal, with no relation to any of the others. By demand of Congress or the administering agencies, every grant was attached to a different set of strings and required separate reports on a bewildering variety of forms. Some called for "comprehensive plans" covering quite different geographic areas, though nobody was sure what happened to these plans once they reached Washington. And, alas, it was a rare local government that could meet these demands honestly. Consequently, many of the applications, plans, and project justifications were highly imaginative. ("Great works of fiction," was the way Robert Weaver, onetime Secretary of Housing and Urban Development, described them to me.) If a mayor couldn't find the figures that those nuts in Washington demanded, he was tempted to make some up and hope that the nuts would never notice.

But somebody did notice, usually, and sent the proposals back for revision. The upshot was that an urban renewal project, say, might take not months but years to wend its way back and forth through the dim corridors of bureaucracy. By the time it finally got approved, all too often the federal money had run out.

In fairness to Lyndon Johnson, it must be said that he did make almost frantic efforts to get the multitudinous federal programs tracking together. As James L. Sundquist points out in his *Making Federalism Work,* for a time LBJ was appointing "a co-ordinator of the month." But since he usually named a cabinet officer to co-ordinate other cabinet officers, and gave him little authority to do anything but appeal to the good will of his jealous co-equals, that never worked. Indeed, all those co-ordinators merely cluttered up the scene still further.

When Johnson began to understand the snarl his administration was in, he appointed a secret task force to tell him how to reorganize the government from top to bottom. Its leader was Ben W. Heineman, a successful lawyer and railway executive, and its membership included such connoisseurs of the administrative arts as McGeorge Bundy, Robert McNamara, Kermit Gordon, and Mayor Richard C. Lee of New Haven.

On September 15, 1967, these gentlemen turned in their final report. It was stamped "Administratively Confidential" —whatever that means—and to this day it has never been released to the public; but as we all know, Washington has its leaks. Within a fortnight, the Heineman Report was the talk of the town.

For it recommended the most radical restructuring of government since the Civil War. It told the President how to get a grip on the runaway bureaucracy. Among other things, it urged him to divide the country into ten federal regions, each with a single headquarters, to replace the "haphazard location of regional boundaries and offices."

These regions, it suggested, would make possible "far more decentralization of operational programs decisions." Washington should concentrate on making policy, and the President's office should be strengthened so it could make sure that the big policies all pointed in the same direction. But the day-to-day responsibility for carrying out these policies, through the states and local communities, ought to be handled in the field by "responsible federal officials—men who can make decisions and make them stick." When hassles arise among the agencies, they should be settled on the spot—that is, within the ten regions—by "field representatives" of the President's Office of Program Co-ordination. Caesar would have called them proconsuls. And indeed they would have deserved that title even more than Ralph Widner in his Appalachian province, because they would have been endowed with more authority over the old-line federal departments.

All this, and much more in the Heineman Report, made eminent sense. It followed the principles of organization used for decades by most successful big businesses. It also incorporated ideas that had been argued—futilely—by generations of management experts in the Budget Bureau, notably Sam Hughes and Dwight Ink. Johnson, I am told, recognized its merits—but in the end, he sent the report off to the archives and forgot about it. He was preoccupied with Vietnam and with rising unrest at home. Perhaps he was already thinking about his abdication. Certainly he had little stomach for another major battle with Congress and the entrenched bureaucracy; a battle which, with his dwindling political capital, he probably could not win. He could count on little public support, because issues of governmental housekeeping—however important—are almost impossible to dramatize. Besides, according to pretty reliable White House gossip, he did not like the recommendation that some federal employees be moved from Austin to a new regional headquarters in Dallas. Big as he was in some ways, LBJ was also a petty hometown chauvinist.

When Nixon took office, one of the few things to which he was clearly committed was more effective management of the government. He resurrected the Heineman Report and had it restudied by task forces of his own. Much of the reorganization he later proposed shows a strong family resemblance to the changes originally suggested by the Heineman group.

On May 21, 1969, he announced the establishment of ten federal regions. Their boundaries are not precisely the same as those recommended in the Heineman Report, but the idea was identical. To the astonishment of some key permanent civil servants, this order provoked little political flak—presumably because he made his move so soon after taking office, and so quietly that the potential opposition never got organized.

Even so, it was a near thing. Daniel P. Moynihan, then a counselor to the President, wrote me in a letter dated November 5, 1970, that "This was a matter that fell within my purview at the time. It was obvious something had to be done, but even more obviously it had to be done immediately. To delay even as far as May 21 (when the announcement was made) would be too long. Unless I am mistaken, the matter was put before the President and he decided to go ahead on about his sixth day in office. Had he waited until the tenth day the reasons for not doing it would have almost overwhelmed him, as they had done each of his four predecessors."

Originally Nixon had wanted eight regions, rather than ten. The biggest would have included all the Pacific Coast states, plus Arizona, Nevada, Alaska, Hawaii, and Guam. (Like most Californians Mr. Nixon apparently thought of Arizona and Nevada as suburbs of Los Angeles.) Another big one would have covered the Rocky Mountain states and much of the Midwest.

Politically, these two superprovinces were nonviable. Senator Warren Magnuson of Washington was one of the most influential men in Congress, and he was not about to let his constituents be subordinated to a federal office in California. He demanded, and got, a split-up of the Western region so that Washington, Oregon, Idaho, and Alaska became a separate province, with headquarters in Seattle. It has been nicknamed, naturally, "Maggie's Region." Moreover, under the original plan Kansas City would have lost a number of federal offices to Denver, the proposed capital of the Rocky Mountain-Midwest region. The alert politicians and businessmen of Missouri descended on Washington and argued persuasively that so big a region would be unwieldy: whereupon four of its states were carved out to form a new region with headquarters in Kansas City.

The people in the Budget Bureau who worked out the nuts and bolts of the new arrangement did not regard it as ideal. They would have preferred to give a special status to certain great metropolitan areas, such as New York, Philadelphia, Chicago, and St. Louis, that sprawl across state lines—making them, in effect, the modern equivalent of the ancient Greek city-states. Under this kind of design, New Jersey would have been cut in half, with the northern part attached to New York and the southern to Greater Philadelphia. But for historical and political reasons, it was deemed prudent to make the provincial boundaries run along existing state lines. The day has not yet come, alas, when it is feasible to vivisect even New Jersey—a state notoriously ill-governed and, when you look at the facts of contemporary geography and population spread, uncalled for.

In the beginning, the new regional system embraced only three departments—HEW, HUD, and Labor—plus two agencies, the Office of Economic Opportunity and the Small Business Administration. These were responsible for most of the welfare and social programs, and after the Defense Department they handled by far the biggest piece of the federal budget. Later additional members gradually were brought into the system: The Departments of Agriculture, the Interior, and Transportation, and such quasi-independent units as the Environmental Protection Agency. More probably will be added in the future, although it is unlikely that the system will ever cover *all* federal activities. There is no logical reason why the Coast Guard and Internal Revenue Service, to mention only a couple, need to be fitted into the pattern.

In two important ways the provincial scheme differed from the recommendations of the Heineman Report. Nixon did not create a new Office of Program Co-ordination to supervise it; instead he tucked it under the wing of the Budget Bureau, later renamed the Office of Management and Budget. Neither did he name a "field representative" of the White House to run each of the regions. Instead he decided on management by committee, a Federal Regional Council, including the local chiefs of all the member agencies. The nearest thing to a presidential spokesman was a liaison man assigned by the Budget Bureau to each of the Councils—and his job was to observe and suggest, rather than to serve as a strong executive officer. Indeed, the Councils have no real executive. One of the members of each is designated as chairman by the President, but he has no staff and no authority to impose a decision on other members.

Of course Nixon and his management specialists knew that this arrangement was merely a dim shadow of the original Heineman concept. They didn't like it, but they decided—probably correctly—that it was the best they could get away with. They well understood the impossibility of getting decisive action out of a committee in which every member exercises a veto. But they understood, too, that Congress would not, at that time, stand for anything stronger. Every member of Congress cherishes his influence with the departments and their field officers. They are his main channels of patronage and power. Usually a field officer is appointed only with the consent of the senior senator in his region and the approval of the congressional committee chairman most interested in his work. Moreover, the executive departments always have kicked against firm supervision by the White House. Neither they nor Congress, then, were willing to tolerate a White House field man with genuine authority. Earlier, in fact, when the Budget Bureau had tried to set up relatively innocuous field offices of its own, Congress had promptly stopped it.

Nobody, therefore, could expect too much from the new federal regions. They are not federal provinces, and they have no proconsuls. But they are still far from useless.

For one thing, a governor no longer has to travel over half a continent, as Ned Breathitt did, to find the federal officials with whom he has to do business. He can now find them in one city—and sometimes he can actually get them together in one room to discuss a common problem.

The Councils do achieve some co-ordination, even though it grows out of consensus rather than command. When ten men sit together twice a month to talk about the problems of their region, they almost always begin to develop a common point of view. They may become a sort of mini-culture. At least they understand what other agencies are trying to do, and usually they will make some effort to help each other. When push comes to shove, of course, they will still pursue their own career motivations, the interests of their separate constituencies, the wishes of "their" Congressmen, and the directives (often rivalrous) of their Washington offices. Knowing this, the Council members tend to avoid issues that might lead to serious conflict, or to buck them upstairs for somebody in Washington to decide. But on less contentious matters, they do seem to be working together much more smoothly than in the old days when they seldom spoke to each other. In some cases they are even coming to look at problems from a regional point of view—as a whole, involving all the agencies and the states within the region—rather than from the narrow, functional points of view of their Washington headquarters.

As such attitudes develop, there is in fact some decentrali-

zation in decision-making. The not too spiny questions can
often be decided on the spot, by bargaining and compromise,
rather than by endless referral back and forth to Washington. The result has been a spectacular speedup, for one
thing, in applications for federal money. Back in 1967 HUD
used to take an average of ninety-six days to produce a yes
or no to a mayor's request for a rehabilitation loan. Three
years later, when the Regional Councils were in operation, it
was able to make up its collective mind in an average of five
days, because most of the interagency friction points could
be handled locally rather than through high-level Washington consultations. For the same reason, it has been possible
to shear away bales of red tape. HUD once required a city
seeking urban renewal money to submit 286 specific items
of information, many of which it didn't really need and
which the city often could not honestly provide. But HUD
felt it had to demand such data because it had no other way
to keep an eye on what was happening "in the field." When
the regional system got working, 137 of these items were
dropped, thus relieving local applicants of nearly 800,000
pages a year of useless paperwork. Similarly, HEW was
able to eliminate fourteen of its required reports and simplify eighteen more, for a savings of 351 man-years of work
annually. And so on through the whole list of agencies.*

What seems to me most significant about the Regional
Councils is their potential for evolving, over the years, into
potent instruments of federal administration. The main
thing needed to this end is the endowment of one man on
each Council—either the chairman or the OBM liaison
officer—with the kind of muscle specified by the Heineman
Report, together with close attention and support from the

---

* The figures cited were given to me by Dwight Ink of the Office
of Management and Budget, one of the fathers of the regional scheme.
They have not been published, but are documented in the internal
reports of the Office.

President's office. The Councils would then be capable, as Martha Derthick put it, of making "federal executive action . . . more expeditious, efficient, and adaptable to needs expressed by particular state and local governments." There were some indications that the Councils already were developing in this direction, until the Nixon administration was engulfed in the Watergate morass. After that the White House had scant attention to devote to such matters.

In retrospect the founding of the ten federal regions may be seen as one of the few enduring accomplishments of the Nixon administration in domestic affairs. That would be in keeping, certainly, with historic tradition. Both in this country and in England most innovations in government have come from parties of the left: Liberal, Labor, and Democratic. Governments of the right—Tory or Republican— have then come along and tidied up. However they may despise the newfangled ideas of their predecessors, from the income tax to Social Security, the conservative regimes almost never repeal them. Instead they usually try to make them work better. They find the flaws that the liberals, in their headlong enthusiasm for change, inevitably overlook; they patch and tinker and overhaul the clanking machinery of government. This is natural, for conservatives by temperament are concerned with the arts of management, to which liberals and radicals pay so little heed. Such conservative achievements are not exciting—but they are not negligible either.

If the federal regions do develop into strong tools of government, they will of course have to win more support from both Congress and the states. This may come more easily than one might expect.

For the country has been groping ever since the Roosevelt era for regionalism in a variety of guises. And these experiments have usually found congressional backing, or at least acquiescence, in spite of Congressmen's inherent suspicion of anything that might weaken their own influence. The reason is that pressures keep building up for regional solutions. Washington is so far away; the states are so weak or so lazy; and so many problems are neither national nor manageable within state boundaries.

The first, and still the best known, of the regional experiments was the Tennessee Valley Authority. Its success in flood control, electric power production, land restoration, reforestation, and revival of the Valley's economic life led to many proposals for duplicating it in other river systems. But it proved to be unique. Its example did lead, however, to regional experiments of two different kinds—each of them, as it turned out, quite different from TVA in both structure and scope.

One group is a series of organizations designed to handle the problems of rivers that flow through several states: flood control, pollution, environmental protection, and the division of waters among competing claimants. The earliest of these was the Delaware River Basin Commission, created in 1961. Unlike TVA, which is a federal corporation with strictly federal control and financing, the Delaware Commission is a joint creature of the federal government and four states: New York, New Jersey, Delaware, and Pennsylvania. Its main job has been to manage the waters of the river—dividing them fairly among the four states, and making plans to cope with floods and pollution. It has not attempted the massive investments in economic development and power production that have distinguished TVA, and it seems unlikely to develop much beyond its present modest scope.

A small sister of the Delaware Commission was set up in 1970 by a similar interstate compact for the management of the Susquehanna. Seven other river commissions have been created under the authority of the Water Resources Planning Act of 1965. They have had little money, staff, or authority, and at this writing have made only moderately successful efforts to co-ordinate the planning of the federal agencies and the thirty-two states with which they are concerned. Only one of them, the New England River Basins Commission, has undertaken any serious planning of its own. Here, as in so many cases we have noted elsewhere, the vigor of the organization can be credited to a single man. He is R. Frank Gregg, a veteran conservationist of exceptional energy and political know-how. Appointed chairman of the New England Commission by President Johnson, he was kept on the job by the Nixon administration, presumably because replacing him would have been politically dangerous. He has managed to dominate even the powerful Army Corps of Engineers. The planning his Commission has under way for the New England rivers and Long Island Sound promises to be of considerable importance; but unlike TVA, it is not chartered to go beyond this one specialized function.

The other family of regional experiments that followed the TVA example is not concerned primarily with rivers, but with economic development. The most successful of these is the Appalachian Regional Commission. In the same legislation that authorized ARC, Congress called for five additional commissions to serve the same purpose in other parts of the country where poverty was pretty rife, though not quite so rife as in Appalachia. The Johnson administration did not really like this idea. It would have preferred to see how the Appalachia experiment worked out first, but for familiar logrolling reasons, it had to go along; too many Congressmen refused to vote for ARC unless they got at least the promise of something for their poor people too.

Not surprisingly, these five regional commissions have never amounted to much. Lacking enthusiasm for them, the Johnson administration never asked for more than token appropriations to support them. Unlike ARC, which is answerable directly to the White House, the junior five were placed under the smothering supervision of the Commerce Department. Their management was entrusted, almost contemptuously, to congressional patronage appointees, rather than to professionals of Widner's caliber. Their boundaries were drawn even more arbitrarily than those of Appalachia. The Coastal Plains Regional Commission, for example, covers a strip along the Atlantic seaboard of three states, Georgia, South Carolina, and North Carolina. As a consequence, the eastern counties of these states belong to the Coastal Plains region, while their western counties belong to ARC—and their middle counties belong to no commission at all. Given this sort of administrative hodgepodge, it is probably just as well that the Coastal Plains region never developed enough muscle to make a nuisance of itself.

The underlying weakness of the five junior commissions is their artificiality. None of them has a strong regional identity, as Appalachia had for generations. Hence they lack political support; many of the people who live in the Four Corners region or the Upper Great Lakes region have never even heard of them. When Nixon decided to abolish them, no articulate public rallied to their support.

Yet strangely enough, they survived. Barely. Congress refused to execute them, although it also refused to give them enough money to do anything except a modest amount of paper planning. Disowned by the executive branch, they were living in 1974 in a kind of limbo. Congress evidently thought that they might someday, under another administration, be pumped up with money and vigor. Meanwhile, their mere survival was one more indication of the persistence of the regional idea.

Another indication was a bill introduced in 1972 by Senators Montoya, Cooper, and Randolph that would have blanketed the whole country, wall to wall, with regional development commissions designed on the Appalachian pattern. It generated considerable initial interest, but faded from sight because of the Nixon administration's opposition and the growing congressional preoccupation with Watergate. At Senator Montoya's invitation, I testified in favor of the bill, because I thought it offered a chance to get some decent regional planning. Later I developed serious doubts, because I don't believe the two-headed scheme of administration, with federal and state co-chairmen, is likely to work well except in exceptional circumstances such as those of Appalachia—and perhaps not even there indefinitely.

The most promising future for regionalism, I now believe, lies with the ten federal Regional Councils. They are at least established, wall to wall. If given a vigorous shove by some future, activist administration they have the possibility of developing into true provincial governments, of the kind Heineman & Co. suggested. I hope I live long enough to see it happen.

The literature on the Tennessee Valley Authority is so voluminous that I see no need to discuss it here. On regional organizations in general, I know of only one good book: Martha Derthick's *Between State and Nation* (Brookings Institution, 1974). An Urban Institute publication of 1970, *Federal Regional Councils*, by Melvin B. Mogulof, gives a thorough though highly technical account of these institutions, with recommendations for their future development. The testimony before the Senate Public Works Committee on the Montoya bill of 1972 (S.3381) constitutes the most far-reaching discussion of the regional idea that I have found anywhere. The full history of the ill-fated five junior regional commissions (or Title V commissions, as they are known in Washington, from that section of the bill that created them) rests in the dust of the Commerce Department files.

14.

Wavelets of the Future

When my wife and I moved to Leete's Island back in the mid-sixties, we did not know that we were part of a wavelet of the future. I was just fed up with working in New York City and commuting to the suburb where we then lived by way of the notoriously unreliable and uncomfortable New York Central. From then on I expected to devote most of my time to writing—among other things, this book. For that, the best place seemed to be a quiet, inexpensive small town. But I had to be within a couple of hours of travel time of New York, where I still had occasional business; and I needed to be close to a good library, preferably with a university attached, so I could discuss the questions that continually crop up in my work with professors, who ought to know the answers. (They don't always, as I soon found out.)

After a couple of years of scouting we finally alighted in an old yellow farmhouse perched on a bluff above the shores of Leete's Island. It fitted our modest budget; Yale University, with the third largest library in the country, was only twenty miles away; and I could get to New York in about two hours, if the Penn Central train was not daunted, as it so often is, by a storm, or a heavy dew.

Certainly it is quiet enough. Four hundred years ago the island actually was one, a member in good standing of an archipelago now known as the Thimbles. The shallows between it and the Connecticut mainland gradually silted up, however, and turned into salt marshes. When causeways were thrown across these marshes to carry a road and the New Haven railway, Leete's Island became, to all intents, a peninsula; but during big hurricanes it turns back into an island again for two or three days at a stretch.

According to the tax assessor, the island is part of Guilford Township, but its residents still think of it as a separate community. Once it had its own school, post office, filling station, general store, railway depot—a shed about the size of a box stall—and liquor shop. Now all of them are gone, or converted into homes, except for the liquor shop, which Noreen Contois keeps open for a few hours every weekday afternoon. Until about fifty years ago the island even had an industry of its own: a quarry where a couple of hundred men blasted out the distinctive pinkish-gray granite that forms the spine of the peninsula. It was loaded directly on the barges for cheap shipment to New York, a hundred miles to the south. There it was used to build such monuments as the Brooklyn Bridge, the base of the Statue of Liberty, and also for street curbings and the stonework in many office buildings, including one where I work from time to time. So even when I am in the city I can recognize migrant bits of my home place.

Since the quarry closed, a victim of reinforced concrete, the island has reverted to farming. From our windows we can see the barns of the Leete place, said to be under the ownership of a single family for longer than any other working farm in America. There Bill and Lawrence Leete raise dairy cattle and cut cordwood on land that came down to them from an earlier William Leete, a colonial governor of Connecticut. He landed in 1639 with the shipload of Puritan refugees who founded the village of Guilford, four miles to the northeast. Their families are all listed in the local records, although the name of the ship—a 350-tonner—somehow has been mislaid. Of the twenty-five names on that

list, fifteen are still common in the township. So much for
the myth of American hypermobility, at least in this neighborhood.*

Our only qualm about our new home was living among
Yankees. When I was growing up in Texas, I learned that
New Englanders are mean-spirited folk, stingy, puritanical,
taciturn, and shrewd. This was received doctrine in a family
that consisted on one side of unrepentant Confederates and
on the other of poor farmers who had for generations believed that they were harshly used by Yankee mortgage-
holders in Boston and Hartford. Now that I've been surrounded by New Englanders for some years, I am beginning
to suspect that such a view—still common throughout much
of the South and West—could be a little myopic. They are
indeed a peculiar people, different in many ways from the
Americans I have known elsewhere; but the differences are
not what I had expected. I am now ready to concede that in
the arts of living together sensibly they are—perhaps from
long practice—a little more skilled than most of us. Indeed,
they may be well on the way toward building the Almost
Good Society, unnoticed. Since our community is fairly typical of hundreds in New England, it is as good a place as any
to observe how they are doing it.

You will not find such communities in western Connecticut. That part of the state, where the brokers and advertis-
ing men gambol and the bloody marys flow, is really a
suburb of New York. Its towns—Greenwich, Darien, New
Canaan, and their neighbors—have been so overwhelmed

---

* The Quinnipiac Indians gladly sold Guilford Township to the
colonists, because for generations they had been fighting a losing war
with the Mohawks and Pequots. At the time of the deal, the Quinnipiac tribe was down to forty-seven men and in danger of being wiped
out by the next Mohawk raid. So much for the myth of the noble
savage, supposedly happy and tranquil until the coming of the whites.

by commuters that the native Yankees have long since been deracinated, or driven beyond commuting range. Today New England begins somewhere east of Bridgeport.

But in the villages of eastern Connecticut—Stonington, Haddam, Deep River, Ivoryton, Guilford—the natives still have the situation well in hand. "What you have to understand about this town," one of my neighbors once told me, "is that it is run by the same people who have been running it for three hundred years." As I have slowly got acquainted with our local ruling class, I've come close to realizing how right she is. Not only do the Old Yankees generally have the last word on most political and economic issues; they also set the cultural and spiritual tone of the community. Today most of Guilford Township's residents are newcomers— Italians, Puerto Ricans, Slavs, Negroes, and Middle Westerners—who have arrived within the last few generations. Yet nearly all of them, within five or ten years at the outside, find themselves engulfed by the Yankee ethic. They think, talk, and behave as if their families had come over with that first ship. The assimilative powers of New England are remarkable.

For example, when Dr. William Arthur Holley died a couple of years ago, he was buried in the Leete's Island cemetery, the only really exclusive institution hereabouts, with the pastor of the First Congregational Church conducting the ceremony. This church has always been dominant in the life of the community; for the first hundred years or so its board of vestrymen was the town's governing body, and its pastor was in effect mayor. We are no longer such a theocracy, but to the friends who came to stand in the April rain beside Doc Holley's grave, it seemed only right that he should leave via the Congregational rites of passage, because he was as pure-quill Yankee as anybody there. Although he was born in North Carolina of Negro parents, he had lived at Leete's Island since 1917. All of his life he had worked hard, got himself an education, acquired his own business—a pharmacy in New Haven—paid his debts promptly, raised his children to be doctors and teachers, saved money, kept up his property, carried his share of civic duties, and observed the local rituals. If anyone had ever called Doc Holley puritanical—a term I've never heard used around here—he would have taken it as a compliment.

While Guilford has had a small black population ever since it was a station on the underground railroad during the Civil War, it has never had a ghetto. Today most of the Negro families are distinctly middle class—a school principal, proprietor of an artists' supply store, supermarket manager, banker—and their homes are scattered throughout the community. The same is true of the Puerto Ricans, who now outnumber the blacks; one of my neighbors raises game cocks. The Puerto Ricans came as migrant laborers, for seasonal work in Bishop's apple orchard and the strawberry and vegetable farms. Some of them liked the place, in spite of its far from tropical winters, and settled down to year-round jobs in brass foundries and other local industries.

Yes, industries. A stranger driving through probably wouldn't notice them. Guilford looks as if it might have been designed by Grandma Moses as the Classic New England Country Town—complete with elm-shaded green, monument to the Union dead, white church spires, tinker's shop, Grange Hall, and lots of eighteenth-century saltbox houses. This appearance is deceptive.

For Guilford, in spite of its Grandma Moses guise, is really a manufacturing town. As of today it has thirty-two factories, making a broad range of products: pharmaceuticals, magnetic wire, conveyor belts, precision tools, flexible tubing, marine hardware, electrical fittings, and laminated identification cards, to mention only a few. Yet it has no "factory district." The plants are dotted at wide intervals

over the forty-six square miles of the township. One occu-
pies a converted trolley barn. Others are tucked away in the
forest or screened by landscaping. (Our neighbor on the
other side of our meadow, Douglas MacLise, does most of
the landscaping; he learned it properly, in Great Britain.)
All of these plants are fairly small, with work forces ranging
from three or four men up to a couple of hundred. Most
produce goods requiring modern technology, or at least considerable skill; wages, as a result, are relatively high. A case
in point is the Guilford Brass Foundry, a mile down the road
from our house. It is a modest shop, no bigger than a good-
sized barn, surrounded on three sides by woods. To my wife
it looked like just the place to take a prized old brass kettle
which needed mending. The manager looked at it with
interest, but shook his head.

"Twenty years ago we would have been glad to take on
this kind of job," he said, "but we can't do it now. We are too
busy catching up on our orders for radar components."

He sent her instead to Tinker Hubbard, an elderly gentle-
man, who could fix anything from a lawn mower to a turret
lathe. Such work was as much a hobby as a profession, since
he came from an old family and owned lots of land hereabouts. The whole town felt it lost a major asset when he
died, well into his eighties, after his motorcycle ran off the
road. His family insists that it was not an accident—he
never had accidents—but probably a heart attack.

A Guilford factory hand can go home for lunch, if he is of
a mind to, on foot or bicycle. He is more than likely to own a
skiff with an outboard motor, which he uses for fishing on
evenings and weekends, and a shotgun for hunting ducks in
the marshes. Oysters, crabs, clams, and mussels are a familiar part of his diet, since they can be had for the taking, in
season, in a dozen bays and estuaries. (I have collected the
makings of an unsurpassable *moules marinières* in ten min-
utes from the tidal ledge below our yard; in a New York

restaurant, it would have bankrupted me.) Anyone who can't be bothered to catch his own fish can pick them up at the town harbor, which accommodates a small commercial fleet. And the three markets offer excellent locally grown meats and vegetables at prices a Manhattan housewife wouldn't believe. Also exotic vegetables, which I can't name, imported from the Caribbean for the Puerto Rican trade.

All this may have something to do with the fact that none of my informants could remember when Guilford last had a strike—although several factories are organized and labor is anything but "docile." (Docility is not a Yankee characteristic.) The men aren't afraid for their jobs, either, because unemployment is negligible. Jobs are going a-begging, in fact, in a number of trades.

That is one reason why the town's welfare budget is only $16,675 for the current year. The other is that hardly anybody is willing to go on the poor rolls so long as he (or she) can lift a hand. I know several grandmothers who are ironing shirts and cleaning other people's homes when they ought to be in bed nursing their arthritis. Such work is not, however, regarded as unrespectable. Nor is any kind of work, so far as I can tell, considered menial or dead-end. On the contrary, a man is not fully respected unless he can turn his hand to almost anything, from rough carpentry to home repairs. Most people actually *like* manual labor, apparently. Chris Neydorff, the high school boy who sometimes helps around my yard, wears his hair fashionably long, but he also holds down several part-time jobs—not from hunger, but because he is saving money for a car and future college fees. Another neighboring youngster, Chipper Griffiths, raises quail and sells their eggs to those few families who occasionally want fancy *hors d'oeuvres* for a cocktail party.

Few, because cocktail parties are hardly part of the local *mores*. The Leetes and some of the other old-timers don't drink at all, and those who do generally pick up a six-pack at

Noreen's and take it home; it's cheaper that way than drinking at a bar, or a party. They aren't stingy, exactly, but they are careful. (Since I'm a close man with a nickel myself, that doesn't bother me.) Not many people around here are either very rich or very poor. Some retired couples on Sachem Head and Old Quarry Road live in houses that suggest they are, in the local phrase, "comfortably well off"; but there are only a couple of really ostentatious homes, and they were built in the Great Gatsby period of the twenties. Their owners wish they could sell them now. On the other hand, there are no slums. The typical dwelling is a modest frame house (like my own) more than a century old. A few of them look cramped or shabby; but nearly all, except those in the center of town, have a little land, often several acres, fringed with sumac and juniper and lilac. Most have a vegetable garden. Both woods and water are within easy walking distance for any active youngster, since two rivers wind through the township and much of its land is in publicly owned forest.

From the externals, it is hard to guess whether a Guilford resident is hard-up or well-off. In either case he is more than likely to wear, on weekdays, denims and Sears, Roebuck boots, and to drive a pickup truck. He uses it for, among other things, carrying his own trash to the town dump, since we don't have a municipal garbage collection service. Even if we did, the pickup would remain popular. Owning a yellow Cadillac may be a status symbol in Hollywood and Houston; here it would be taken as proof of thriftlessness, bad judgment, and worse taste. When he gets a little money ahead, the Yankee would rather invest it in the stock of a local bank, or timber acreage in the north part of the township, which is appreciating steadily in value.

Garbage collection is not the only municipal service we do without. Since Guilford has no sewerage systems, and water lines only in the town itself, most households depend on wells and all of them on septic tanks—ecologically the best of all means of waste disposal, if soil and drainage conditions are right. Where they are not, our health officer, Dr. Elisabeth Adams, will not let you put up a house. Because much of the terrain is either granite ledge or marshes, overcrowding therefore is not an imminent peril. Any number of other services normally performed in the city by paid employees are handled here by volunteers—the fire companies, visiting homemakers for the elderly and invalid, the park and recreation commission, the zoning board, the Keeping Society which looks after historic houses, the library building committee are the ones I know best. A Land Conservation Trust and the Audubon Society acquire properties that should be kept as open space. The Leete's Island Garden Club built and maintains a small park, as well as the window boxes around the town square. The West Woods Trail Association marks and keeps clear some thirty-five miles of footpaths through our main forest. A recycling committee, made up largely of high school kids, collects and sells old newspapers and bottles; the proceeds go to the fire companies and a school for retarded children. And so on. Anyone willing to serve finds himself co-opted quickly to work on at least one of these innumerable volunteer groups that keep the community going.

What services must, of necessity, be handled by officialdom are more efficient than I have known anywhere else. Soon after we moved here a rainstorm clogged up a culvert under our road and sent a small flood streaming into the garden. When I asked Doug MacLise what to do about it, he said, "Why, call Milton Bullard, of course." Mr. Bullard was then our First Selectman—in effect, the mayor. He answered his own phone at once, and said he would see what could be done. No promises; but before midafternoon the town engineer had unplugged the culvert. Only someone accustomed to the sluggish labyrinths of New York bureaucracy can understand how miraculous that seemed.

Our present First Selectman is Marge Schmitt—twice unprecedented, in that she is both a woman and a Democrat. She and the two other selectmen, and everybody else at Town Hall, can't help but know how their bosses feel about any given subject, even before it comes up at town meeting. They talk to a good share of us every day.

For Guilford is still small enough and stable enough to be a true community. Everybody knows everybody else, or feels he does. Personal, responsive government is still possible. Moreover, nearly everybody is infected with a lively concern for the present state of the town, and its future. We know that it has to grow, because no place within the Atlantic Urban Region can escape the population explosion; but we hope the growth can be channeled in an orderly and rational fashion. Hence Guilford's "Comprehensive Plan of Development," adopted after many months of study and debate in town meetings. It anticipates a doubling of the population, to about twenty thousand, by 1985, and it provides in advance for the necessary schools, roads, open spaces, and public buildings. To my amateur eye, it is a thoughtful piece of work—an ingenious accommodation of tradition and change. The towns I knew out West all wanted to grow as fast as possible, and welcomed any new business from a slaughterhouse to a striptease joint. Not Guilford. By common consent, it encourages only those firms that are "consistent with . . . the community character" and then only when "subject to strict controls on nuisances and pollution."

"Common consent" is not always arrived at harmoniously. I have seen old friendships broken up by such explosive questions as the design of the new police station. (Should its architecture be modern or phony-Colonial? The phony-Colonialists won, and their opponents, including most of the resident architects, are still fuming.) And Bill MacLise complained for months about the iron heel of tyranny, because the zoning board would not let him build a marina on his West River property.

When an issue does get decided, it usually has been discussed until it is frayed at the edges, in our weekly paper, and in the bank lobby, and at Page's hardware store. Agreement is finally reached because busy men—company presidents, Yale professors, and Al DeBay (who, being a carpenter, is probably the busiest of all)—devote their considerable talents to community affairs. The conclusion that emerges—right or wrong—is pretty much the sense of the meeting. This, I guess, is what is meant by "participatory democracy." An exhausting exercise, but bracing.

Guilford is not very different from a hundred other small towns in Connecticut. But Connecticut is very different from the other forty-nine states. It reminds me of Switzerland more than any other place, because it never had any natural resources to speak of, aside from scenery and timber. Even its topsoil was mostly scraped off by the glaciers and dumped eighteen miles out at sea, to form Long Island. So, like the Swiss, the people who settled Connecticut have always had to make a living by importing raw materials, fabricating them as far as their ingenuity would go, and then exporting them at the highest possible price. Again like the Swiss, they pioneered in the making of timepieces, armaments, and other metalwork. (During the Middle Ages, Switzerland was famous for its armor; Connecticut is famous for its guns, helicopters, and aircraft engines.) Both places specialized in trades that demand little except pens, paper, and character: banking for the Swiss, insurance for Connecticut.

Both also have avoided overcrowding. When you fly over Connecticut, most of it looks like wilderness or farming country. But this is a happy illusion. Actually it is densely populated—more than five hundred per square mile—and a larger percentage of its people are employed in manufacturing than in any other state. Yet its three cities—Bridgeport, Hartford, and New Haven—are relatively small, because so much of its manufacturing is scattered among small towns like Guilford.

Historically, this can be explained by three Yankee characteristics: ingenuity, a sometimes cranky individualism, and a hankering for elbowroom. The ingenuity led to more patents being granted to Connecticut citizens than to the residents of any other state, in proportion to their numbers, from the founding of the patent system in 1790 until the thirties. They included the stagecoach and Sam Colt's revolver, which together opened up the West, and Eli Whitney's invention of interchangeable parts, which made possible the Industrial Revolution. As individualist, the New Englander preferred to run his own business if he possibly could, even though he might make more money working for somebody else. This is still true; the number of one-man enterprises, many of them marginal, is astonishing to anyone who comes from the corporate world.

The instinct for elbowroom resulted in the scatteration. Two examples. A sea captain, long in the African trade, laid aside a few elephant tusks after each voyage. Eventually he had enough money to start a comb factory. By 1809 he employed twenty artisans, and later he expanded his product line to include billiard balls and piano keys. Today plastic has replaced ivory as feedstock, but the industry still thrives—not in an established manufacturing center, such as Bridgeport or New Haven, but in the tiny village of Ivoryton, where Captain Phineas Pratt preferred to start it.

If you have ever used witch hazel for a sprain, sunburn, or shaving lotion, you have patronized the main industry of the little town of Essex, the E. E. Dickinson Co. So far as I can learn, it is the only distiller of witch hazel extract in this country. Unlike most of the state's factories, it does not have to import its raw material, since hazel twigs grow in abundance along the Connecticut River and in nearby marshes. But who except New Englanders would have believed that a successful business could be founded on such a source, or in such a place?

One reason why Connecticut industry prospered from the beginning was its location, midway between the metropolitan markets of Boston and New York, both easily reached by sea. But today the Connecticut pattern of manufacturing in small, livable communities can be duplicated almost anywhere, thanks to the interstate highway network that has freed industry from dependence on rail and water routes.

And there is some evidence that this already is happening. The small town, which seemed to be dying in the fifties, began in the next decade to show signs of a rather remarkable revival. This was most visible in the South, the country's latest fast-growth area. In a study of 4,641 southern towns of less than fifty thousand population, Calvin Beale, head of the Department of Agriculture Population Studies Group, found that virtually all of them grew during the sixties by two-digit percentages. Even the smallest—those with fewer than five hundred people—grew by 15 per cent, as compared with a bare 5 per cent in the previous decade.

Perhaps more significant is the change in public attitudes toward the small town. As James L. Sundquist noted in a 1973 paper on population dispersal:

"All public opinion polls taken on this subject in this country and abroad—especially in France which has apparently done more polling on this subject than anywhere else —show that the public has a marked preference for smaller communities. The most recent authoritative poll in this country is the one taken for the Commission on Population

Growth and the American Future. They found that only 55 percent of the respondents were satisfied with the size of the communities in which they lived. Of the other 45 percent, most would prefer to live in a smaller place. And in the very large cities, only 39 percent expressed satisfaction.

"On the question of whether the federal government should discourage further growth of large cities, the nation-wide vote was 52 to 33 in favor of that proposition. An interesting aspect was that the residents of the large cities voted in about the same proportion—51 for and 36 against —as the population as a whole."

As Sundquist also pointed out, Great Britain, France, Italy, the Netherlands, and Sweden all have firm programs for relieving the congestion of the big cities and encouraging migration to smaller communities. To make such a policy work they have used a wide range of devices: the building of new towns; subsidies to encourage industry to move to less crowded areas; public investment in roads, schools, utilities, and port facilities; and rigid controls on the use of land. In much of Great Britain, a landowner cannot put up a factory, office building, or even a home on his own property without government permission.

In America we have no strong national programs for dispersing population, and I doubt whether we ever shall have in the foreseeable future a land use policy as tough as Britain's. So far Congress has refused to act on much weaker administration proposals for guiding land development in the public interest. But in our usual piecemeal, pragmatic fashion we seem to be moving slowly in the same direction as Western Europe. In 1970 President Nixon called for policies that would "not only stem the flow of migration to urban centers, but reverse it"—although in his preoccupation with Watergate and the threat of impeachment, he did nothing to follow up his declaration. In the same year Congress committed itself "to a sound balance between urban and rural America" and called for a biennial presidential report on progress to that end. So far Congress too has failed to pursue this commitment, and the White House has not got around to even the first of the requested reports. But in the meantime a growing number of organizations—the 1972 Democratic platform committee, the National League of Cities, the National Governors' Conference, and the Advisory Commission on Intergovernmental Relations—have come out in favor of some kind of national growth policy that would spread our population around more evenly.

In the absence of a clear national policy, both local and federal governments have been moving—haltingly—to resurrect the small community. We have had some public encouragement, with money behind it here and there, for new towns. The Appalachian Regional Commission and its five less vigorous sisters have all tried to stimulate the development of small growth centers. So have the local development districts. And in the medium-sized cities, such as Minneapolis-St. Paul, Jacksonville, Atlanta, Seattle, and Indianapolis, the movement toward more effective metropolitan government has encouraged growth there, rather than in Megalopolis. The same is true in suburban communities, such as Westchester and Nassau, which have created effective forms of countywide government.

Up till now the march has been a slow one, without national celebration. Yet it still inches ahead, by means of all the social inventions touched upon in this book. It offers a reasonable hope, I believe, that we may someday reach the Almost Good Society—and the goal may be closer than the despairing daily headlines lead us to think.

Index